T0198722

Slave Scripture

A Protocol Manual for the
Owner and Owned

NORMAN MCCLELLAND

authorHOUSE®

AuthorHouse™
1663 Liberty Drive
Bloomington, IN 47403
www.authorhouse.com
Phone: 1 (800) 839-8640

Published by AuthorHouse: 03/16/2018

ISBN: 978-1-5462-3409-8 (sc)
ISBN: 978-1-5462-3407-4 (hc)
ISBN: 978-1-5462-3408-1 (e)

Library of Congress Control Number: 2018903453

Print information available on the last page.

Slave Scripture:
A Protocol Manual for the Owner and Owned

by the Thrall[1]

Someone who thinks that a man who chooses to erotically submit to another man is less of a man is someone who has a very limited understanding of manhood.

> "Whisper Master of all you'll do to me,
> My heart to beat in expectation of.
> Drive me to madness with your voice and touch,
> And tantalize with blissful agony.
> Make me a raging fire of your lust,
> Which cries in suffering to be put out.
> Toy with my soul 'til I no more can bear,
> Just as the cat plays cruelly with the mouse.
> Take hold of me like a taloned eagle,
> And as that beast, I beg my life consume.
> Plunge me into a tortured ecstasy,
> That is a death of self while yet alive."[2]

---

[1] Thrall is Old English for *slave* and is the name his own Master Lynn calls his slave of twenty-three years.

[2] By the Thrall.

Contents

Chapter 1

Master/Slave Relationship: What Is It?

A Master/slave[3] relationship is different from other relationships in that it functions through an elaborate set of rules (protocol) that to most in the non-Master/slave community will seem ridiculous and at times even disturbing. However, for those in the Master/slave community, such protocol serves to create a bond between the Master and slave, the intensity of which will not be found in any other relationship.

This Master/slave protocol is itself different from most slave protocol manuals, in that it is written by a v-slave and not a Master. Even some of the best protocol manuals written by Masters, as might be expected, have only a limited understanding of what goes on in the mind of a slave, which is very different from what any Master may imagine.

> The mind of a Master
> Is not that of a slave.
> What the first does not know
> Could not fit in hell's cave.

What is a v-slave? A person who feels empowered by volunteering to make most of his own wants and needs secondary to the wants and needs

---

[3] For many in the leather community, it is felt all terms of dominance (Daddy, Dom, Master, Owner, Top) should always be capitalized, while that of submission (boy, sub, slave, owned, bottom) should be in in small letters unless the word begins a sentence. This is the way these terms are found in this book.

1

of another (the Master) and who agrees that if he or she does not do so, the Master has the right, in some previously agreed-upon manner, to punish the slave—physically or non-physically. Being a slave is not the same as thinking one *wants* to be a slave. No one is a slave until he has served under a Master, which just might cure him of wanting to be a slave.

Naturally, this leads to another question: what is a Master? This is a person who feels empowered by convincing another person (a slave) to voluntarily make the slave's wants and needs secondary to that Master and is given the right by that other person to punish him or her in some previously agreed-upon manner if the slave does not follow through on his or her slave status. However, a Master also has been recognized as a Master by his peers and is able to keep a v-slave for an extended period of time. What a Master is *not* is a petty dictator. He is not someone who feels empowered by controlling others against their will.

Please note that most of the experiences of this author have been with male Masters, Doms, slaves, and subs. He has had occasional interactions with female slaves of male Masters, female slaves of female Masters (Mistresses), and male slaves with female Masters (Mistresses), but he does not know enough about their inner dynamics to legitimately judge how much his experiences can be thought to match theirs; he suspects that the will to obey is genderless.

This protocol is dedicated to my current Owner, Master Lynn Sipe. I owe all of the detailed slave protocol that is found below to the following individuals and organizations: the other Masters I have had and known; the slaves and subs I have known and played with; the founders of the Punishment Club LA; the founders of the slave rap group LA; my once-upon-a-time submissive (Boston); the uniform/leather club Trident International, Los Angeles; the SM club Avatar, Los Angeles; and the National Leather Association, Los Angeles.

Chapter 2

The Law

When it comes to the Master/slave issue, the obvious should be noted, namely the Thirteenth Amendment to the US Constitution (1865). That amendment abolished slavery and involuntary servitude throughout the United States, except as punishment for a crime. However, it says nothing about "voluntary" slavery. Naturally, such v-slavery has no recognition in the law and is exclusively a part of the power-exchange subculture.

Chapter 3

Slave Protocol

Protocol is a code of correct conduct or set of rules and acceptable behavior used at official ceremonies and occasions. It is closely related to and overlaps with etiquette, which is also a set of rules for acceptable behavior. Etiquette is what most people learn as they grow up and is usually less ceremonial than protocol. What follows is called *slave protocol,* although much of it could be called *slave etiquette.* But whereas etiquette might be observed wherever one went and with whomever one interacted, protocol is generally observed in more limited places and with a more limited group of persons.

Very little of the following protocol is oriented to those who only have a desire to play the slave once in a while in a one-night stand. For those players, slavery is a fantasy game for guys who know that as soon as the game is over, they can return to the safety of being independent and free to do as they please—until the next time they want to play slave. Serious slaves never *play* at being slaves, for they wish to be nothing more than slaves and see being independent and free to do as they please as unsatisfying. This protocol is for those who are genuine slaves and their Masters.

As one should expect, there are many misconceptions about being a slave, and we will deal with these throughout this manual. Let us start with the most critical one. The core of a person in slavery is not sadomasochism, bondage, erotic discipline, non-erotic discipline (punishment),[4] or playing with sex toys. All these are peripheral to any real sense of slavery.[5] Instead, a slave's core consists of adopting a certain ritualized lifestyle of self-disciplined behavior. This may include how, in the presence of his Master or even when not with him, the slave speaks or does not speak; how he stands, walks, sits, and kneels; how and what he eats or does not eat; what he wears and does not wear; where he sleeps (beds down); how he distinguishes his limited needs from unlimited wants; how he puts another person (the Master) before himself; and how he relates to those outside the Master/slave (M/s) relationship. All of this ritualized behavior is called *slave protocol,* which at times includes a counter Master protocol. In other words, the purpose of slave protocol is to keep the slave, as much as possible, aware that he is a slave.

Protocol keeps both the Master and the slave with a sense of connectedness not possible otherwise. For example, if in a restaurant a slave can sit wherever and however he wishes, he has no reason to remember he is a slave. However, if he is always required to sit on a certain side of his Master, to sit only before or only after his Master sits, to be eating only when his Master is eating and not before or after, etc., the slave is in constant awareness that he is a slave.[6] For the true slave, this awareness is not a burden but a joy.

There are three levels of slave protocol practiced in public or private. At level 1 (low or invisible protocol), the slave observes only that protocol that can easily be disguised (made invisible in public) as non-slave related. For example, the protocol of slave street dress is observed; he wears what

---

[4] For the purpose of this manual, the word *discipline* will mean erotic discipline, while punishment will mean nonerotic discipline. See more on this below at Chapter 23. Punishment.

[5] Most of the following applies to a female slave with a male or female Master/Mistress.

[6] See Chapter 12. Public and Private Eating Behavior.

appears to be a vanilla (seemingly fashionable) chain collar;[7] he always is walking and if possible sitting with the Master on his preferred side, but he does not kneel before his Master; he does not obey extreme slave speaking/silence protocol; he calls the Master by what appears to be a nickname that does not add the word *Master* or *Sir*. This low level would be observed when the Master and slave are in any environment where more intense protocol would catch unwanted attention. Low protocol may also be used when attending family and non-kinky friends' events. With modifications, it may be the protocol used at home in private, although the full collar would be worn, the Master would be called *Sir*, and the slave would be expected to be nude, if those were the standard rules. On the other hand, during private sex play, part or all of the full or high protocol (level 3 protocol) might be required.

At level 2 (medium) protocol, the slave observes the standing, walking, sitting, and clothing protocol but still does not kneel or obey extreme slave speaking/silence; however, he wears an obvious collar and uses the word *Master* or *Sir*. This level would be observed in a public environment that is more tolerant of atypical behavior.

At level 3 (high) protocol, the slave observes all the proper standing, walking, sitting, kneeling, speaking/silence, and clothing protocol, including the full collar and possibly harness. Here the slave's total attention is on his Master's body and will. This protocol is not used outside of the kink Scene (environment).[8] Obviously, high protocol is less often observed than the other two.

---

[7] Vanilla: This term, at its most basic, refers to sex between a man's penis and a woman's vagina and little if anything more. However, in the past few decades, it has been expanded into the same-sex community to mean simple oral-genital, genital-anal, or oral-vaginal sex and little if anything more. In other words, in the either the heterosexual or homosexual community, it refers to non-kinky sex.

[8] The word "scene" when capitalized (Scene) refers to the general Leather/Kink, SMBD Community, or Master/slave Community. When not capitalized, "scene" means a particular play session between two or more Dominant/submissive (D/s) or SM players involved in a physical and psychological interactions in which there is a power exchange.

Chapter 4

Definitions

Terms the reader may need some insight into are *Top, Daddy, Dominant (Dom), Master, bottom, boy, submissive (sub), servant, S&M (sadomasochist),*[9] *BDDSSM (bondage-discipline-dominance-submission-sadism-masochism), Owner/owned, the power exchange* or *the leather/kink community,*[10] and *Master/slave (M/s) rituals and contracts.*

A Top is nothing more than the individual who, during a sexual encounter or relationship, receives oral intercourse (a blowjob) or is the penetrator during anal intercourse (fucker). A bottom is generally any individual in a sexual encounter or relationship that gives the blowjob to (fellates) the Top or is the receiver in anal intercourse (gets fucked). Some men regard themselves as exclusively Tops or bottoms and cannot or will not switch. Most Tops and most bottoms will, however, under the right circumstances, go the other way. This includes when two horny Tops compete (playfully fight) with each other to determine who is going to do what to whom, or with two horny bottoms; whichever one can switch the easiest will be the Top.

It is a common belief in the gay community that there are ten bottoms

---

[9] The use of the & between the S and the M has gradually fallen out of use and been replaced with a simple SM; this simpler form will be used from now on in this book.

[10] This is a catch-all term that includes those who not only find it erotic to wear leather, but rubber, latex, and military/police-style uniforms. From now on, this will usually be shortened to simply Leather Community.

for every Top. I do not know where this number comes from, but there certainly are more bottoms than Tops, so anyone who can switch has an advantage. It may be easier to be a bottom than a Top because less is expected of one. Many bottoms think that a Top should automatically know exactly what a bottom wants. This puts a lot of pressure on the Top, and a disappointed bottom is often willing to be critical of the Top who did not read the bottom's mind and satisfy him. In short, bottoms can be crueler than Tops. Another reason there are fewer Tops is that good ones need training, and it is hard to get that. Bottoms do not generally need training. A third reason for the scarcity of Tops/Doms/Masters is that many of those who have the potential and who might lean to the sadistic side are frightened of that side; and rather than learn to accept it in a safe, sane, and consenting way, they sublimate it into masochism. As a result, what might be a good and well-demanded Top/Dom/Master spends his life as a bottom or submissive who will never be satisfied. One indication of this is the number of times a sub or slave, once he has learned that his Dom or Master's SM needs and wants can be challenged safely and sanely, develops the confidence to transform himself from a sub or slave into a Dom or Master.

That the titles Top, Dom, and even Master are not rigid is further shown by the Top who will bottom for a specific activity such as getting flogged by his bottom, unless he prefers to use another Top. This lack of rigidity is likewise found in the bottom that, although rarer, will only top in a specific activity such as pissing on another bottom or even more rarely on a Top.[11]

Something that must be made clear is that the term *bottom* should not be equated with the term *submissive* or vice versa, any more than a Top is automatically a Dominant or Master. This is because one man topping another man does not automatically mean that the bottom considers the man behind the dick in his mouth or up his asshole to be an authority figure of any kind, and there are any number of times that a Top has taken

---

[11] A Master may piss on a submissive as a declaration of ownership, as a dog pisses on his territory to signal his right to that territory. Some Masters may be so toilet trained as to be unable to piss directly on their slaves, but this can be overcome by him pissing in a cup and tossing that at the slave.

himself too seriously in relation to a bottom, only to experience the bottom laughing at the Top.

As a Top has the complement of a bottom, a Daddy has the complement of a boy; but before going further, it needs to be made absolutely clear that this second complementary pair (D/b) may have nothing to do with the age of either of the individuals. While in the majority of cases, a Daddy is older than his boy, in a few cases, the younger male (or female) [12] takes on the parental status. Even less often does the age issue usually enter into the Dom/sub (D/s), or Master/slave (M/s) pairing. It is true that a minority of Masters feel comfortable only with slaves younger than themselves; however, since slaves are difficult to come by, most Masters will gladly take on slaves older than themselves. In fact, as a teenager, and well before becoming a slave, this author was a Dominant to a much older submissive.

Of all the above pairings, the Daddy/boy seems to be the most common. Among the main reasons for this are: (a) a D/b concept is a more familiar one for most people; (b) it requires far less extreme (radical) psychological adjustment than an M/s one; (c) it is more socially acceptable to both the general gay and straight community; (d) it is easily open to the love and romance that most people are looking for, and (e) it does not imply any SM in the relationship. Even if D/b spanking scenes might be part of the relationship, that scene is so widespread in the nonkinky community as to hardly qualify as SM. [13]

Another clarification that is needed is that the term *submissive* and *slave* in their respective D/s and M/s pairing are not identical. While all slaves are automatically submissives, all submissives are not automatically slaves. In fact, most submissives are *not* slaves and will never be. Slaves are actually a rather tiny minority of submissives.

Some in the D/s community believe that submissives can be grouped into three main categories: (1) the psychological submissive, who tends to seek out pain and humiliation more than anything else; (2) the sexual submissive, who finds full sexual satisfaction only in a submissive role, but outside of the sexual scene has no real submissive inclinations; (3) the

---

[12] There are women in the kink community who assume Daddy/boy (spelled boi) relationships.

[13] See 53. First, the Heavy Hand

natural, true, or full submissive, who outside of any scene-specific event craves to submit to a Dominant. This is the only submissive that makes for a real slave.

In the case of the natural slave, once his submissiveness does manifest itself, and if he is fortunate enough to receive top-notch slave training, he will find it relatively easy, or even totally natural, to feel fulfilled as a slave, although not necessarily automatically as a 24/7 one, which is a rarity.

It also needs to be emphasized that the term *submissive* is not to be equated with *passive*. Few Doms want subs who offer little or no response to the Dom's sense of being in charge. Such passives are sometimes called "Do-me-queens" and are far more interested in what the Doms can do to and for them than in what they can do for the Dom. This is not to be confused with "Force-me queens" who are subs and slaves who trying to force their Doms/Masters to do something to them. A subcategory of this "Force-me" slave is the slave who, before he will serve, demands to be "broken" like a wild horse. While a few Masters will go for this, most do not want to spend the time or effort to do so when they can get a more compliant slave.

The opposite of a passive sub is an active one, in which the sub will actively do things to and for the Dom, such as performing really good oral sex on him, rimming him, licking his boots, maybe even massaging his back and/or feet, or if the Dom has some masochistic needs, the active sub tries to satisfy them.

A final misunderstanding about a submissive, non- slave, or slave, is that he automatically has a submissive personality. The fact is that a submissive may have a very dominant personality, and he often becomes a submissive to balance or even seek relief from the heavy burden of that personality.

Before we go further, we need to return to the title of boy. While the title "boy" is always the complement to the title "Daddy," it is also used as a general synonym for any male (and sometimes female) sub or slave. However, in a true Daddy/boy relationship, "boy" has no necessary submissive connotation; in fact, there are even Daddy/boy relationships in which the boy is the more dominant of the two. In other words, calling someone a boy in a Daddy/boy relationship is a term of endearment.

Calling a sub or slave a boy, on the other hand, does imply a full submissive or subordinate status with no necessary endearment involved.

Caution: the use of the term *boy* as a reference to a submissive or slave is to be confined to very specific situations, such as with a man's Dom or Master or someone who has directly or indirectly been given permission to use that term by the Master or by the slave himself. A Master other than one's own may use it in front of the boy's own Master, as in such utterances as "And this must be your boy," but not otherwise without his Master's permission. Instead, he would say "sub coy" or "slave coy."

For example, I attended a Master/slave gathering in which I showed up before my Master. A Master who knew me noticed I was standing alone, and although talking to another Master I did not know, signaled me to approach him. I got within arm's length of him, assumed the proper slave stance—that is standing tall, chin in, feet slightly parted, and both hands behind my back—while waiting to be recognized, since the slave is never supposed to be the first to speak to a superior. The first Master asked rhetorically, "The boy's Master isn't here yet?" He had every right to assume that, because I would not have been standing alone away from my Master. He also had the right to refer to me as "boy," since he was a Master known to my Master and this slave.

"Right, sir!" was my reply.

He then turned to the Master he had been speaking to and said, "This is Master Hal's boy."

The second Master acknowledged this boy with a nod of his head and the word "Boy."

Without having received any permission to respond except minimally for the purpose of politeness, I returned the nod and said, "Sir!"

In this case, everything was properly done. The known Master had the right to use "boy" as long as he tagged my Master's name to it. The second Master had "received" the right to call me "boy" from the first Master, but only on the assumption that he was shortening the phrase "Master Hal's boy."

In situations other than this, the slave may indirectly give his permission for the use of "boy" when he wishes to make his sub status clear to a Dom/Master; for example, "Sir! This boy is pleased to meet you." Also, slaves who know each other, especially if they are friends, can call each other "boy." Thus, when a Master introduces his slave (boy) to another Master's slave (boy), the slaves can acknowledge each other with "boy." A non-alpha slave, however, does not refer to a training alpha slave as "boy," but as "Sir!" or as "Alpha" (slave), unless the two slaves are on very friendly terms.[14] In all of this, it needs to be emphasized that the use of *boy* in the above allowed-for contexts is regarded by the boy and the Dom/Master as a direct empowering of the Dom/Master and an indirect but equally empowering of the boy.[15] Beyond this, the term *boy* will usually be regarded as a put-down, and the person inappropriately using it might find a boy's fist in his face.

To summarize the differences between a Daddy/boy and a Master/slave boy, a Daddy's boy and any other non-slave boy does not follow the rigid slave protocol found here. For example, a non-slave boy does not follow the very specific standing and greeting protocol of slaves, is not required to kneel[16] at his Dom's feet, and is more or less free to speak and dress as he likes.[17] Also, negotiated compromises are much easier in a non-slave/Master relationship. For example, in my one attempt at being a boy to a Daddy, the latter wanted me to shave off my beard. When I told him I was too attached to it to lose it, we found a compromise. He shaved off all my pubic hair, making me look absolutely prepubescent "down there." Rarely would such a compromise be found in a Master/slave relationship, and if found, the compromise would be harder on the slave.[18] Since I much prefer the Master type over the Daddy type, it was only a one-time shave.

What has been said above should not be taken to imply that a Master and a Daddy are totally separate categories. There are relationships in which a Dom will be the Master to a slave and a Daddy to a boy. In these relationships, the slave will usually not have any real need for a romantic relationship with the Master who, if he wants that without giving up his slave, may also have a boy who will offer him that romantic element. This triple relationship (Master/Daddy, Master's slave, Daddy's boy) works

---

[14] See Chapter 48. Alpha Submissive/Slave.
[15] See Chapter 24. Empowering Humiliation.
[16] See Chapter 9. Hand Shaking; Chapter 11. Kneeling Procedures; Chapter 10. Standing Positions
[17] See Chapter 15. Slave Wear II.
[18] See Chapter 21. Hair.

well if all involved respect each other's status and jealousy can be kept to a minimum.

My personal experience in such a triple relationship, however, was not positive. I had contracted with a Master as his slave, but with the hope for a romantic component to that relationship; as far as I was concerned, our relationship was working fine until the Master wanted to add a second person into it. It wasn't that I objected to a third party, but the addition was, without a doubt, a boy-toy who was never going to be a real submissive. This was proven by the fact that he resented taking orders from me as the senior (alpha) bottom. In fact, he made it absolutely clear that he regarded a slave as lower than a free boy-toy. I repeatedly asked the Master for backup on this matter, but what I got was only lip service, since a boy is not usually open to being punished. Naturally, this made me wonder if the Master didn't share that boy's evaluation of me. Finally, I rebelled.

After a three-way shouting match, the Master took off his belt, shouting at me to drop my pants and get down on all fours. This time, it wasn't just that I resented his taking the boy's side, but he was now demanding that I be punished in front of the boy-toy. A slave can be punished in front of another Master or another slave, but not in front of a boy-toy. Proper protocol required that the Master either order the boy out of the room or that the boy should ask and receive permission to be excused. Clearly, neither was going to happen, and my anger would not allow me to demand it. If the Master was going to violate protocol like that, I was going to use it as ammunition for what I knew I would soon do. I just stood there defiantly staring at the Master, but then he yelled, "Slave," and the slave, still blazing with hostility, did as he was expected to do. I dropped my pants, got on all fours, and received more than I was expected to tolerate if this were an erotic scene. As I took my punishment, I reconnected with my sense of slavehood, and a state of submissive calmness came over me.

After that, the Master dropped the issue, but I could not. I was not prepared to simply walk out on the contract and allow the Master—or worse, the boy-toy—to defame me, so for the next two weeks, I became passive-aggressive, doing things or not doing things that required punishment until the Master finally realized I was going to tire him out with this and asked what I wanted. I told him I was not willing to cope with it anymore and requested that either the boy leave or that our contract be dissolved. The Master made the choice. The boy-toy stayed, while the slave was given his freedom. That, however, was not the end of it. Without a slave to discipline, the Master began to treat the boy-toy as a boy slave, and that never works out. The Master thus found himself without slave or toy.

I have to admit that part of the problem was mine. First, because the boy-toy was satisfying the Master's romantic interests, I was being denied that, which I resented. Second, while the boy-toy may have thought of himself as superior to a slave, this slave felt that since he was willing to commit far more effort (discipline) to the relationship than any boy-toy needed to do, this slave was superior to the boy-toy.

The slave versus boy-toy issue brings us to an important component in the life of any slave, which is non-erotic discipline or punishment, which, it must be emphasized, does not automatically mean physical pain.[19] While many slaves are masochists, many others are not. To be a slave, be he a masochist or not, involves a far more complex mind-set than that of just Dominance/submission, bondage/discipline, SM, or any combination of these. However, before we go into this greater complexity we need to define that generally controversial term "sadomasochism."

Sadomasochism is one of the most difficult terms to define because it means so many different things to so many different people that any simple attempt at a definition is more or less meaningless. The common definition is that of one individual (the sadist) getting off on giving what most people regard as pain, while another (the masochist) gets off on receiving what most people regard as pain. It should be obvious that this is such a vague definition that it is almost useless, because it is absolutely relative. One person's pain is not another person's pain, but it can even be another person's pleasure. If two or more people are playing with belts and paddles, whips and canes, etc., what determines that this is SM versus heavy or rough vanilla sex? A fair answer is the players themselves, and only they, have the right to determine this.

It should be no surprise that those outside the Scene are rarely satisfied with this right of the people in the Scene to define SM. Any sexuality that is not that of the majority in society is always considered suspect, which usually means morally perverted and/or mentally unhealthy. Leaving aside

---

[19] See Chapter 23. Punishment.

that it is for religious fundamentalists' simply satanic sinfulness the rest of society tends to view SM in one or more of three ways. (1) It is the playing out of society's patriarchal oppression or internalizing and then projecting out all the cruelty of that oppression. (2) It is the internalizing and then projecting out of the child abuse that all the participants must have experienced. While both of these reasons undoubtedly apply to some in the Scene neither reason is as universal as most people would like to believe. We will deal with more of this later on.) (3) The masochist at least is trying to somehow escape from his own body as some religious ascetics try to by punishing the body he hates or rather having another (the sadist) do so for him. Interestingly, this same claim has been made about people who are really into tattooing, branding, or otherwise modifying their bodies.[20]

If you ask most of those receiving the pain (the masochists), they will tell you that it is a way to get more deeply in touch with their bodies; the tattooed person will often tell you the same thing.[21] If asked for more specifics, they will usually give one or more of four reasons for their masochistic orientation.

(1) They are striving for the endorphin high brought on by the body dealing with pain.

The bottom who is going down this endorphin path may not even be interested in genital sex, as it may interfere with or distract the high brought on by pain.

(2) They are into SM for what they regard as one or more psychological (mental health) benefits. This can actually include what some players regard as a constructive (healthy) way to deal with some child-abuse history. This may or may not go along with therapy sessions with a therapist who is supportive of the Scene.

(3) They are into it for playing with what they consider the dark side of human nature, which most people try to suppress, but in a safe, sane, and consensual way. Even a one-night stand SM

---

[20] See Chapter 22. Tattooing and Other Body Modifications.

[21] It should be obvious that tattooing is not the same as undergoing cosmetic surgery because the individual does not like the shape of his or her nose or breast size.

requires a self-revealing honesty rarely necessary in a vanilla one-night stand. This honesty automatically creates an intimacy between the Dominant and submissive that is a major reward in itself. The fact that the submissive has "trusted" the Dominant to take control of that submissive empowers that Dom; and the willingness to offer up that trust gives power to the submissive. This trust can give both players a high that is not found in non-SM experiences.

(4) They are seeking some intense spiritual experience that goes beyond what most established religious groups can offer. There is, in fact, a whole gay and lesbian SM subculture called Black Leather Wings, which is dedicated to the use of SM for spiritual purposes. This often involves many primitive religious elements.

None of these four SM reasons needs to be exclusive, and while the majority of SMers probably start out with only one of them, many discover the others and may even abandon the original reason for one or more of those others. This is especially true if one of these reasons is better than another in leading the participant, especially the bottom, into an altered state of consciousness (ASC) that may include a powerful out-of-body experience. Here the experiencer, especially for a slave, may have allowed his sense of self or his ego to be so absorbed into the self or ego of the Dom or Master, even if only temporarily, that the sub or slave feels he has so little psychological ego left that he no longer even feels pain personally. In other words, any such pain experienced is only as something disconnected from him and thus not really his pain. Not all slaves have this extreme sense of merging with the Dom or Master, but every sub with the right Dom or Master will experience, to some degree, a merging, and this should give the Dom or Master a major sense of rewarding power. In fact, the consensual BDSM and Dom/sub or Master/slave Scene is mainly about power, and anytime pain is involved, it is as a servant of that power, *not* as its master.

Clearly, most of those who are likely to call themselves SMers do so to distinguish their activity from "just rough sex." So, in general, SM players are those who, as bottoms or Tops, after a fulfilling scene experience a heightened sense of personal power and thereby self-worth and who hope their partner experiences an equal sense of heightened power and self-worth, hence a power exchange. This sense of power may continue for hours or even days, until a new scene is needed.

This positive definition of an SMer would exclude those who suffer the "after-rebound syndrome." This is a sense of remorse, fear, guilt, and self-loathing that some experience after really kinky sex. Since this syndrome is rarely found in a supportive S/m relationship, it will not be further dealt with here

The most important message about SM practice is that if giving or receiving pain is equated with trying to harm someone or be harmed by someone, then the average SM Top and bottom should not be into giving or receiving pain. The goal of most SM "play" is to use radical physical and/or mental stimulants to ensure that the bottom and Top experience a level of pleasure not gained by more conventional bottoming and topping activities. Of course, none of this is to say that there is not a minority of individuals, bottoms and Tops, who are looking to harm and being harmed, but that is a tiny minority in the SM Scene; harming and being harmed can equally happen in vanilla scenes if that is the intent of the participants.

To be even more specific, the consent-requiring sadist must be clearly distinguished from the non-consent-requiring sadist. The latter is not interested in giving consensual pain but nonconsensual pain. In other words, the real sadist is not into any mutual power exchange, so from now on, the use of the term *sadist* will refer only to the consensual-power-exchange sadist.

Actually, in a purely dominance/submissive situation, there need not even be a physical SM component, because the dominance and submission could be totally psychological in nature. The Dom is able to use his verbal and body language, which may include a strong element of power or erotic humiliation, to make the sub completely under the Dom's control. This may be as kinky as things get, because it may be followed by nothing more than Top/bottom vanilla sex.

One thing should be understood: in the majority of SM relationships, there is no element of dominance/submission, much less Master/slave "authority." The average SM bottom does not regard himself as submissive to the Top. What the bottom is seeking is the pain/pleasure; he is not seeking to be dominated. Similarly, the Top does not regard himself as a dominant over the bottom, in which case the pain/pleasure has no erotic disciplinary element, much less a non-erotic (punishment) element.[22] Even a simple (non-slave) submissive, masochistic or not, is still an equal to the Dominant in most things. This is especially true in an adversarial SM relationship in which there is both an aggressive sadist and an aggressive masochist.

The lack of any intense "authoritarianism" in the majority of non-SM Dom/subs, SMers, and SM Dom/sub is because most are "scene-specific role-play." This means that when a particular scene is over, both players regard each other as equals in all ways. The reason for this is that most of the individuals in these scenes have no interest in taking on a long-term authoritarian status and the responsibilities that this entails.

In contrast to either a strictly non-SM Dom/sub or SM Dom/sub, there is little to none of the elaborate protocol found in the Master/slave relationship. For example, a non-slave sub may not even wear a collar, or may do so only during play at home. But a slave, to signify he is owned, wears a collar as much as is practically possible, which often means even hidden under his regular outside clothes, because now the Master has the right to demand obedience from the slave in and outside of a scene.[23]

Another way of saying the above is that in a non-slave SM relationship, the bottom or the sub has the right to complain if the Top or Dominant is not giving the sub what he wants, while in a Master/slave relationship, the Master technically decides if the slave is going to be satisfied, the slave technically has no right to demand this from the Master. If the slave thinks he has that right, he is no longer a slave. A contract, of course, will change this, in that both parties are under the authority of the contract.

This contract authority, more than anything else, is not only what distinguishes a simple Dom/sub relationship from a Master/slave one, but the reason why Dom/sub relationships are so much more common than Master/slave ones. A contract automatically "limits" the freedom of a Master in relationship to his slave, since the Master as much as the slave is

---

[22] See Chapter 24. Empowering Humiliation.

[23] As might be expected, there are some couples who will play Master and slave in a scene, but as soon as they leave the scene, they are equals. This is not the real Master/slave Scene.

ruled by the M/s protocol. Most Doms do not want to give up the freedom to live independently of their sub, which a Master must do as he and his slave "live dependent" on each other. Naturally, this interdependency leads to the question why any Dom would become a Master. The answer is simple: what freedom the Master gives up is compensated for by the much greater right of power he has over the slave than the right of power the Dom has over the sub.

To put the above differently, the Master/slave relationship is completely bound up with the authority position that is at the core of that relationship. This means that in every genuine Master/slave relationship, the authority component is manifested in a punishment element, although this need not automatically involve pain, especially since there are an infinite number of painless punishments that a creative Master should be able to come up with.[24] This means there does not need to be any traditional sadomasochistic element in the M/s relationship. Even if punishment need not be pain oriented, I challenge those few individuals who have said that there need not be any punishment element in a Master/slave relationship.

This author has known of only one M/s relationship, if it can be called that, in which there was theoretically no punishment involved. One of the men was in his early twenties and the other in his late twenties. The younger had the label of slave and the older the label of Master. The slave was always naked at home and never sat on the future (two common but not universal slave traditions).

I asked the Master, "Do you ever have your slave do what he doesn't want to do?"

"I love my slave. Why would I want to make him do something he doesn't want to do?"

"Never?" I asked.

"Well, sometimes, but we work it out."

"How?"

"We usually compromise."

"Does your slave ever want to do something you don't want to do?"

"Sometimes."

"What do you do then?"

---

[24] See Chapter 23. Punishment.

"The same. We compromise."

"Do you ever punish your slave?"

"Of course. He likes to get spanked. And I like doing it."

"Is one of you more on top than the other?" I asked.

"He [the slave] likes to bottom, so I always Top. I'm the Master."

I won't go on with this dialog, because I think as short as it is, it makes several points. (1) "Compromise" is not a word one expects to hear from a Master, because that is not submission to a Master's will. (2) Punishment is not kinky sex that a slave likes. (3) Being on top because the slave prefers the bottom does not determine a Master; giving the order as to who is on top or bottom does. (4) Also, because someone wants to be nude and not sit on the furniture, simply because they have heard that this is how slaves are supposed to be, does not automatically make anyone a slave. Also, no one is a genuine Master simply because he wants to call himself that or even because someone who fancies himself a slave wants to call some Top his Master. A genuine Master is someone who has earned that designation and is accepted as such by other Masters.

It has been this author's experience that those punishment-free relationships have been where the slave is mainly someone who does all the housework, and what sex may be involved may or may not be particularly kinky. This author considers such relationships as more Master/servant than Master/slave in nature.

It is true that what one person calls a servant or sub another may call a slave; however, in the most traditional sense, a slave implies "A person who is owned by and labors for another person" (Master) under "the threat of punishment." A servant, on the other hand, may, at worst, be verbally chastised for poor performance, but generally, the only real punishment would be a loss of pay or being fired. This implies that a Master/slave relationship is one of power exchange, while that of a Master/servant is, if any, far less so.

Let me make this clearer still. In the power exchange subculture, some slaves do not labor for their owners as domestic help (servants) but are slaves only in a sexually submissive way, while sharing all domestic activities with the Master.[25] In other cases, it is common practice to make the slave responsible for the maintenance of the Master's erotic wear, especially his boots, for any power-exchange toys or dungeon space. If the slave lives with the Master, this responsibility could even be extended to making and unmaking the Master/slave bed as an extended play space.[26] The slave may take care of the Master's laundry, cooking for and serving the Master his meals, and keeping his (erotic/play) social calendar. In other cases, a true household slave does far more, but whether minimal or maximal in their servant responsibilities, if they are not done properly, the slave will receive punishment.

There is still another way of separating a true slave from a servant submissive. A slave can perform one of four actions: (1) He does what he wants to do and what the Master does not care about one way or another. (2) He does what he wants to do and what the Master also wants him to do. (3) He does what neither he nor the Master wants to be done but nonetheless needs be done. (4) He does what he does not want to do but the Master wants him to do.

In any relationship, M/s or non-M/s, couples are faced with the equivalent of these four; for example, in number four, the wife hates camping but goes because the husband wants her to; or the husband hates the opera but goes because his wife wants him to go.

When a slave submits to a Master, he basically says that as far as number four is concerned, "If I want to do something that you do not want me to do, I will not do it" and "If you want me to do something that I do not want to do, I will still do it."

Furthermore, unlike in the non-M/s situation, the submitter (slave) has agreed inwardly (within himself) and outwardly (with his Master) that he will hold no resentment to doing what the Master wants, not what the slave wants. Thus, in theory, a slave may never need any kind of punishment, but submission is rarely so ideal. This so-called always-compliant slave is the type most likely to be taken for granted, and no slave will tolerate this for

---

[25] A sex slave qualifies more as (personal) property than does a domestic slave. In this author's present relationship, both Master (Owner) and slave (owned) scrub the kitchen floor, etc.

[26] Unless the slave is not allowed to sleep in the bed but must sleep on the floor.

long. This means that he will at some point make his displeasure known, which will be a challenge to the Master's authority, and even though the Master may acknowledge that the rebellion was justified, he will have to punish the slave or leave his authority open to question.

Most Masters, however, will probably not start out with such an ideally compliant slave but one with more self-assertion, and this Master will have to start out with the clear statement, "You (the slave) will do as I (the Master) want, not as you want, and if you do not do what I want, I will punish you."

Naturally, when it comes to the issue of slave discipline and punishment, most people are likely to think "abuse," but in the context of a mutually fulfilling Master/slave interaction, there should be no place for abuse. The reason for this should be obvious. Unlike in true slavery, where the slave has no rights, the voluntary slave allows himself to be punished mainly because it enhances the relationship between the Master and slave.

The best way to understand the difference between slave punishment and abuse is to look at the short- and long-term results. If done right, the slave ends up with a feeling of buoyancy and exhilaration, followed by a feeling of relaxation and self-fulfillment. Abuse never feels good, even if it is completely voluntary. It may relieve for a while some sense of guilt or shame, but it does not make you feel better about yourself or anyone else. In fact, it will always feed back into one's sense of worthlessness. If any slave should have mixed feelings—good and bad—with regards to the self, then he or she should carefully examine those feelings, preferably with a counselor to help separate those feelings and get rid of the bad ones. If he cannot, then he should withdraw from slavery. Moreover, any potential Master should want to avoid him at all costs.

It must be remembered that an authentic Master is one who is in command of himself and thus wants to attract to himself a slave who wants to obey him. That is a slave who wants to share in that Master's self-commanding power. The pseudo- or abusive Master does not really care whether the slave wants to obey and gets his sense of power by trying to force a slave to obey.

Another reason punishment need not equal abuse is that it does not necessarily involve pain. In fact, if the slave is a true masochist, painful punishment is a contradiction, and real punishment would consist of depriving him of pain. The fact is that most of the punishment a slave will receive will consist of little more than requiring him to getting down on his knees before his Master, acknowledge his offense, beg for the Master's understanding, beg to be pardoned,[27] and promise to be a better slave in the future. At the other end of the punishment spectrum, some version of temporary exile may be the deepest pain. The bottom line is the good Master never uses punishment simply to inflict pain.

A further insurance against abuse in a healthy Master/slave relationship can be achieved by the Master asking the slave what he (the slave) feels would be the appropriate punishment. The true slave will never try to take advantage of this by choosing too little a punishment, but will always choose what he knows he deserves.

While in theory, the Master has the right to punish the slave at will, that is even if he has done no wrong, if overdone, this would keep the slave in such a constant state of anxiety that he either would become too neurotic to be an efficient slave or he would bolt from the relationship. In most Master/slave relationships, however, there is a well-established middle ground. The Master with even the perfect slave (a myth) who never does anything wrong, nonetheless, may occasionally feel the need to remind the slave of the Master's authority by a mild, otherwise undeserved punishment. The limits of this should be specified in the contract.

This mild, technically undeserved punishment will rarely cause the sincere slave of a skillful Master to bolt, especially when he knows that his "skillful" Master will soon find some way to reward his slave for this technically unfair punishment, because the Master who does not periodically reward his slave for acts of exceptional submissiveness will soon find himself without a slave.[28]

Again, this is the opposite of abuse, as it clearly shows that the Master respects the slave for his loyalty. A Master who does not respect the right

---

[27] *Pardon* is a better word than *forgive* for a slave to use, as it has more of a dominance quality to it. Also, if at no other time, it is during an asking for the mercy of the Master that the slave should drop using the first-person pronoun ("I" am sorry) and replace it with the third person ("this slave" is sorry, or even better "This slave begs your pardon, Sir") to show absolute deference to the Master. See Personal Pronouns.

[28] See Chapter 23. Punishment.

to proper treatment of his slave is a Master who will lose both the respect and loyalty of his slave and end up with a bad reputation in the M/s community.[29]

When the issue of abuse within an M/s relationship arises, there is an automatic tendency to focus almost exclusively on the Master as the abuser, but the fact is, a slave under the right circumstance can become abusive of his Master. This usually happens because the Master has made a poor choice in the type of slave he has adopted, and by the time he admits that to himself, it may be more difficult to un-adopt (dump) the slave than may be commonly thought.[30]

Naturally, any association of an M/s relationship with the issue of abuse is reinforced by the close association of slavery and sadomasochism (SM), so it is important to examine this association.

Whether non-Master/slave or Master/slave SM Scene, it is probably true there is a higher percentage of individuals who have experienced some sort of child abuse than in the general public. Furthermore, there is no doubt that many SM bottoms try to voluntarily recreate some of this abuse, in the hopes of somehow undoing their past and finding acceptance and even love; and with the right Top, this may actually work. For those bottoms for whom it does not work or does not work sufficiently, they need to leave the Scene and/or seek out supplement trauma counseling.

Childhood abuse, however, is not exclusive to many bottoms. Many Tops into SM are also trying to work out their own traumas. If it is because they have come to identify with their former abuser, they may have an attitude of *I give to this bottom what I got.* Once again, if this Top can find a suitable masochistic bottom, this may work; but more often than not, this Top is in need of even more counseling than a bottom. Neither for the Top nor the bottom should the playroom be a therapist's office.

None of the above is to be interpreted as all SM bottoms and Tops are victims of past abuse or are in need of psychological help. Most are not, and their kink is conducted in very safe, sane, non-abusive ways.[31]

---

[29] See Chapter 25. Slave Pride and Master Pride.

[30] See Chapter 43. Maintaining a Relationship.

[31] It should be obvious but will be stated anyway. Most victims of childhood abuse do not end up in the SM Scene. If they did, that Scene would be many times larger than it is.

As noted earlier, in none of the above slave types is the sadomasochist (power exchange) element sufficient to make someone a slave. The slave-making element is the "authority element." Whereas a simple power exchange element is in force during play scenes between any Dom and sub, it is not in force when the sub is functioning independently of the Dom. In other words, that element of dominance does not cross over into the outside world. The authority element, on the other hand, is in force with or without the Master being present, which means it does cross over into the outside world. How far or how much it crosses over should always be clearly stated in the Master/slave contract.[32]

The importance of this crossover must not be underestimated, because for the man or woman for whom being a slave is not a part-time game but an authentic lifestyle, every reminder that he or she is a slave brings a sense of fulfillment and happiness.

That the authority element rather than any SM, erotic discipline, or nonerotic discipline (punishment) element is what differentiates an M/s from a non-M/s relationship can be seen from the fact that slavery requires behavioral and communicative abilities that can only be described as a ritual process, which is described here as *slave protocol.* In particular, the slave must be constantly aware of the need for differential speech and speechlessness; what he can and cannot wear; how he undresses or is undressed; how he stands, sits, and walks; with whom and how he can have physical contact; how he may have to relate to family members, non-M/s friends, and even his coworkers and boss; how he handles his finances; and how he uses the restroom at home and outside, and otherwise behaves in private and public. In other words, being a genuine slave involves altering one's behavior to satisfy another person (the Master) to a degree not found in a non-M/s relationship.

To summarize, a Master/slave relationship is one in which there is a true authority relationship as well as a power exchange one, which is not normally associated with a simple Top/bottom (T/b), Dom/sub (D/s), or

---

[32] See Chapter 6. Use of the Master's Name; Chapters 14 and 15. Slave Wear I, II; Chapter 10. Standing/Sitting; Chapter 13. Restroom Use; Chapter 35. Family Situations; Chapter 37. Outside Work; Chapter 38. Finances.

SM relationship. Also, in a non-Master/slave relationship, there is generally no need for a formal Master/slave contract.

There is one more pair of terms that can be added to those that have so far been mentioned, which is the Owner and owned. Some in the Master/slave community believe that an Owner and owned can be distinguished from a Master and slave by saying that whereas a Master and slave have a contract under which they both must function, an Owner and owned have no such contract, but in all other ways have an M/s relationship. This lack of a contract technically gives an Owner far more authority (power) over the owned than a Master has over a slave. While this does not automatically mean an Owner/owned relationship is going to be more open to abuse than an M/s relationship, the very fact that a Master has signed a contract with a slave implies that the Master recognizes certain limitations on his authority. The noncontract Owner offers the owned no such limitations. Another way of saying this is that contract-oriented slavery is conditional slavery, which says a slave is such only under the conditions of the contract. Slavery without a contract is unconditional in that the Master (Owner) has unconditional authority over the slave (the owned).

For this author, the distinction between a Master/slave relationship and an Owner/owned one is false. A Master is synonymous with an Owner and a slave with the owned, so I would recommend that any M/s relationship without a contract find a different designation, and from now on, any mention of an Owner/owned implies a contracted M/s relationship.[33]

Please also note that this author does not recognize the concept of a true slave as one who is so only for a one-night stand or a weekend affair. This is playing at being a slave. In something that short, the slave enters into a simple Dom/sub get-together. Also, it is a foolish slave who agrees to submit to an unknown Master before meeting him for several hours of an honest verbal interview. While this interview may be followed by a hands-on session, it is still best not to assume that this is the Master of your dreams. Contract negotiations should be conducted over no less

---

[33] For a different opinion about a Master versus an Owner, see *Beyond Obedience* by SlaveMaster and slave 7 in Further References below. This work divides slaves into noncontract or born slaves and contract or performance slaves.

than a month's time. Remember that an owner without a slave may be as desperate as a slave without an owner.

Regardless of the exact meaning of Owner and owned above, the owned is synonymous with property, and if the term *slave* is a controversial one to the general public, referring to another human being as property is even more so. However, the reality of the human species is that we are very territorial, and property is a part of what we are. This is proven by the fact that in an M/s relationship of any duration, the slave will come to think of his Master as being as much the slave's property as the slave is the Master's property, and the Master who fails to understand this is naïve. I have found that the most intense bond between a Master and slave develops when the Master realizes and accepts such mutual ownership.

The bottom line of the word *owned* is that it signifies a far greater sense of belonging than any non-ownership. It is not only being part of something greater than the self, as in any relationship, but being part of something more powerful than the self. To be owned by another is to give up ownership of oneself and in doing so to surrender an agreed-upon sense of responsibility to oneself to the owner. This is perhaps the major appeal of being a slave, of being owned.[34]

The issue of ownership leads us to another major misunderstanding about a slave, namely that he is trying to become a nonperson, and while that may be true for a tiny minority, the majority of slaves are trying to become even fuller persons than they feel they are as nonslaves. This is actually the complement to the majority of Masters, who feel that they are completed only by having a slave. This makes any slave a very valuable piece of property, which is why very few Masters are into any kind of abuse of their property.

Of course, the problem with all the terms we have covered is that none of them is absolute. For example, there is the Alpha Dilemma, where someone who acts as the authoritarian (Top, Dominant, Master; the Alpha) may like to get fucked or even flogged by his bottom, sub, or slave. In fact, I had one Dominant (not Master) who after flogging or otherwise

---

[34] The words "agreed-upon sense of responsibility" is important because in a legal system that does not recognize true slavery, the v-slave is still legally responsible for himself and all his actions. To disregard this fact is an absurd fantasy.

disciplining me would sometimes feign being very tired and, without any words between us, lie down on the bed on his belly and pretend to be half-asleep. At that point, I was allowed (expected) to fuck him. The absolute rule here was that neither of us spoke about it, during or afterward. It was understood by both of us that it never happened. A second Dominant (not Master) I played with a lot enjoyed getting fucked, but to make sure it was understood that he was always in control, he would either (a) have me on my back, hands restrained to the sides of the bed, while he sat on my dick, doing all the necessary work; or (b) put me in handcuffs and leg irons while he lay on his belly and made me do all the work. In other words, a bottom can be a Dominant. A third Dominant and also Master would order me to fuck him, but since he regarded this as a gross violation of Top/bottom status, he would soon after require me to submit to punishment for my violation of him. Obviously, this was unfair, but he knew the rule that if a Master unfairly punishes a slave, that Master must make up for it by later giving the slave a desired reward (compensation) or at the very least offer the slave punishment credit.[35] Also, I have known several Doms and Masters who enjoy getting fisted and demand that their subs or slaves fist them without any sense that the status of the two is compromised.

I repeat, what determines the dominant and submissive status is who gives and who takes the orders. If a particular Dom enjoys getting fucked, he can order his sub to fuck him. This is referred to as a case of the Top ordering from the bottom.[36] Also, there are cases where two Tops find each other so hot that, after fighting or not fighting for dominance, one will ride the other.

Even if the most uncommon relationship is where the Master bottoms and the slave Tops, all that really matters is that both parties find their satisfaction in whatever arrangements they make. Sexual roles that are fluid are usually the most satisfying.

An interesting example of this fluidity involved a bisexual Master who had a male and a female slave. In this triad relationship, the roles of Top and bottom overlapped, in that the Master would have the male slave fuck the Master, and then the Master would fuck the female slave. In this

---

[35] See Chapter 23. Punishment.
[36] Not the same as topping from the bottom.

threesome, each understood his or her status, and the slaves worked well together—so well, in fact, that the Master at times wondered who was really in charge. I felt sorry at times for the Master, because it was obviously a situation that allowed the two slaves to manipulate him easily; however, everyone seemed happy with the relationship, which is all that mattered.

Remember, a slave is not automatically a bottom, but one who does as he is ordered to do, which may be to bottom or top.

Naturally, all this bottoming of a Dom or Master is a very touchy issue in the Dom/sub and Master/slave community and never much publicized or admitted to. Not only must the Dom/Master find just the right sub or slave that is willing and able to act as the sometimes Top; but that slave must be trusted enough to keep the matter private. Once again, whoever is ordering the action is the Dom or Master, and the one who obeys the order is the sub or slave. This is the essence of the power exchange and/ or authority element; and it is more than either a simple Top/bottom or Daddy/boy relationship. In those relationships, one person simply likes to fuck more than get fucked, and vice versa. Moreover, even in the simple SM power exchange, there is no necessary authority or punishment element.

To blur the Top/bottom lines even more, there is the situation of a dominant masochist and a submissive sadist. In this seemingly contradictory case, while it is the sub who is the pain giver (sadist) and the Dominant who is the pain receiver (masochist), the sub only gives the kind and degree of pain demanded by the Dominant, which eliminates any commanding creativity on the part of the sadistic sub.

This dominant masochist and submissive sadist is not the same thing as topping from the bottom.[37] This latter phrase signifies a bottom, sub, or even slave, who while wanting to still identify as such, tries to control a scene or even a whole relationship because he has a more dominant personality than the Top, Dom, or Master. While there are a rare number of Doms and Masters who like the challenge of taming pushy and resister (fighting) bottoms,[38] if their games are carried too far, one or both players

---

[37] Noir the same as a Top ordering from the bottom.

[38] Not to be confused with a "brat" or a submissive who likes to rebel in a childlike way to get the Dom's attention. Brats are common among the subs in spanking scenes.

can easily get hurt, and unfortunately, one or more bad experiences with such a power-hungry bottom can ruin a perfectly good Top, Dom, or Master. Again, to distinguish a d/m and s/s from the "topper from the bottom," the first retains the respect of the kinky community, while the second does not unless it is only a temporary situation.

The reality is that everyone has to start somewhere, and unless a Top, Dom, or Master has come up through the ranks (started out as a bottom, sub, or slave), he will probably be clueless on a lot of topping things and may need an experienced bottom, sub, or slave to guide him through scenes until he gains the confidence and know-how to be a true Top, Dom, or Master. This is "guiding from the bottom," and no honest bottom wants to do this on a regular basis; however, even after this guidance stage is finished, the "active slave" recognizes that there are always things a slave can teach his Master, as there are always things that a Master can teach his slave. This is called *mutual growth*. Naturally, such growth has its risks, in that instead of the Master and slave growing toward each other, they grow away from each other.

Unfortunately, some novice Tops, rather than learning from experienced bottoms, allow their insecurity to lead them to abusing their bottoms, and if this becomes a set pattern, the Top will never learn how to be a confident Top.

Of course, the growth one experiences as a Top or bottom can actually lead to a reversal of roles, in or outside of a relationship. The easiest of these reversals seems to be a bottom or sub becoming a Top or Dom, or even a slave becoming a Master. Going the other way seems harder for an individual because of a seeming loss of rank versus a gain of it.

Nonetheless, a further sign of the non-absoluteness or relativity of all of the above terms is the fact that, while not very common, a slave can be the Master to another slave. This is not to be confused with an Alpha (top-ranking) slave training a gamma (bottom-ranking) slave of a shared Master.[39] Even rarer is that one Master may have his own Master. These blurring of the lines is often the result of the slave growing into being a Master and the Master growing into being a slave.

---

[39] Some Master who do not accept the training of a previous Master will insist on a new slave being considered a gamma. See 48. Alpha Slave.

The next term that needs to be dealt with is that of the bossy bottom. This is a bottom who sometimes tries to run the Master/slave relationship from below, which is not to be confused with the dominant masochist mentioned earlier. In a Master/slave relationship, to be a bossy bottom or a pushy sub/slave can be debilitating to that dominance/submissive situation, and only initial and periodic punishment may be able to counter that. Many Masters cannot cope with a pushy slave under any circumstances, but other Masters like them. It gives the latter justification for periodic punishment, even though the slave has done no wrong otherwise. This is *not* an excuse for a Master to simply brutalize a slave, and any slave who allows that has more than a serious self-image problem. Each party knowing the safe and sane limits is what keeps the Master/slave relationship loving and not pathological; but within these limits, for the slave not to accept, indeed not to want, this punishment is to be an insincere or pseudo-slave. Of course, as mentioned earlier, in some cases, the worst punishment a Master can impose upon a slave is to "not punish" him, as in withdrawing all but the most minimal acknowledgment of the slave's existence. For a true slave, such indifference is harder to take than any slap, belting, flogging, or other pain-administrating action.

Nonetheless, even for the Master who appreciates a slave's bossiness, it is important that the punishment must remind the slave that such bossiness is at the Master's pleasure, not the slave's.

While bossy bottoms, pushy subs, or slaves may not be on the list of requirements that most Tops, Doms, or Masters are seeking, there is one case where such bossiness is at the very top of the list, namely when dealing with a shy Master.

It may seem a contradiction that a Top, Dom, or Master would be shy, but it is far commoner than is thought. Once the Top and bottom are together in private, the Top's shyness usually disappears, but that is not of much use for initiating the processes, which is where a bossy bottom is useful. Of course, the internet has made such encounters much easier for the Top, as initial anonymity helps protect from possible rejection. Still, many shy Tops still prefer the old-fashioned bar scene over technology.

Before leaving the subject of what makes a Master and what makes a slave, it has been my experience that one thing every slave should be aware of is that within every Master, no matter how well hidden, there is a self-indulgent child who wants his (or her) desires satisfied at a moment's notice. If this is not done or is frustrated for too long, the Master will have an adult or not-so-adult temper tantrum, which can be scary. Therefore, it is the responsibility of the brave slave to subtly act parent-like in dealing with this child element. The slave who cannot manage this will find himself in a less-than-satisfying relationship.

Chapter 5

Why Be a Slave?

Since wanting to be a Master is usually accepted in society as a more natural power urge than wanting to be a slave, the first question that needs to be asked is *why does someone want to be a slave?*

While no one is born a Dominant or a submissive, a Master or a slave, the inclination to be a submissive, but not necessarily a slave, seems to develop rather early in life, even if it does not fully manifest itself until many years into adulthood.[40] While I may not have been born a submissive, my earliest experience of wanting to submit to a man was when I was four years old, and I can still remember the excitement when he playfully slapped my ass.

Some in the D/s-M/s community believe that submissives can be categorized as (1) the psychological submissive who tends to seek out pain and humiliation more than anything else; (2) the sexual submissive who finds full sexual satisfaction only in a submissive status but outside of the sexual scene has no real submissive inclinations; (3) the natural, true, or full submissive who, outside of any scene-specific event, craves to submit to a Dominant.

Any of these three categories can be further classified as primarily pet slaves, working slaves, and show slaves. The first rarely labor for the Master and are kept for the kind of companionship and emotional support that

---

[40] For a different opinion about being born a slave or being slave-born, see *Beyond Obedience* by SlaveMaster and slave 7 in Further References below.

a doglike worshipful attitude toward the Master might offer, but at the same time, this is a slave who craves the attention of that Master and who is easily depressed if he does not get it. The second is a servant-slave and is happy as long as he is kept busy and so requires less personal attention than the pet. The third is more the public slave than the others, since his Master keeps him to show off or display in front of others. This slave may have little tolerance for work, as he will think it beneath him. Each of these three will likely overlap to some degree with the other two, and so this is a very flexible division.

There are, of course, many reasons for a submissive in any category to want to be or at least *claim* to want to be slaves, but of these reasons, several stand out.

(1) There is the person who is more or less looking for an SM relationship, but more hands-on than a scene-specific one.

(2) There is the person who has very low self-esteem and thinks that the lowly and/or humiliating status of a slave will confirm that image of himself, which he is unfortunately very attached to.

(3) There is the person who wants to be taken care of, physically and emotionally. This is especially true of those whose lives are not working out and think that turning responsibility for their lives over to another (a Master) is a solution. Also, this person may include individuals who are unable to develop stable personal relations with others and want an authority figure (a Master) to take care of that for them. However, very few Masters want a slave who cannot function on his own and expects the Master to function for him. This wannabe slave wants to be a slave from weakness and should be avoided at all costs, because if a Master were to give him any responsibility, he would feel betrayed, and when the Master—hopefully sooner than later—dumps this person, he can go into a potentially dangerous rage. This wannabe might be more the boy looking for the Daddy, except the D/b relationship has too much freedom, which is to say that it leaves too much personal responsibility to the boy that a slave is seen as not having or having much less of. So only a Daddy who is looking to take care of a very immature boy would be interested in him. Just to avoid any misunderstanding on this issue, there

is nothing wrong with a slave needing to be taken care of; that is a natural part of every human being, but a slave should also be ready to take care of his Master if that may become necessary.

(4)   Then there is the wannabe who thinks he can get someone to take care of him financially. This is the most deluded of all slavehood seekers, since the number of Masters who are rich enough to support an unemployed slave are few and far between.

(5)   Finally, there is the person who has a great deal of self-confidence, has no need for someone to take care of him since he can do that himself successfully, but who actually wants to be able to let go of his intense feelings of self-control ("I am too much in charge of my life") and seek slavehood as a form of freedom from a significant part of that. How much surrendering of such self-control or how much freedom the individual is seeking will range from mild to extreme, from part time to full time. This is the person who seeks slavery from a position of strength and is the ideal choice for most Masters.

A potential slave can actually fall into more than one of these categories, of which the most common seems to be a Daddy/boy-Master/slave combination. This can start out as the first and evolve into the second or start out as the second and evolve into the first, but it rarely remains both equally.

Chapter 6

Use of the Master's Name/Title

An aspect of slave protocol training is to try, if possible, not to use a shortened form of a Master's name, as it implies a familiarity akin to equality of status. There are some exceptions, as with one of my Masters, who insisted I call him Master Hal rather than Harold, because he hated that name. However, I would never call him simply *Hal*. The same was true for another Master, Abe Sir! Failure to properly address the Master should always be a punishable offense.

Upon meeting a Master for the first time, a slave should give his name to a Master, but only upon request, without asking that Master his name unless it seems imperative to do so, and then only with such politeness as "Sir, do I have permission to ask your name?" However, this does not automatically mean that the slave should presume to use that name in further conversation. As just noted above, such use of a first name, in place of "Sir," suggests a level of equality between the Master and the slave. This is another example of the difference between a Dom/sub and a Master/slave. In the former, more familiarity is usually acceptable.

My personal take on this naming or addressing issue is that since all sorts of people (family, friends, and business associates) may call a Master by his legal first name, this leaves that name without any special significance for the slave. However, to refer as much as possible to the Master as "Sir!" or "Master XXX" creates a significant and valuable verbal bond between the slave and Master shared by no one else.

There are times, however, when the use of Master or Sir will bring too much attention to both Master and slave; still, just to give in to public pressure can reduce the power relationship between the Master and slave, in which case an alternative may be welcomed.

One of the easiest alternatives is for the Master to have a name used only by his slave(s) and if appropriate, used by the slaves of other Masters. For example, the Master may have the slave call him by a word in a foreign language that means *Master* or *ruler* such as Arabic: *Amir, Malik, Sahib* (commander, king, Master); Greek: *Kurios* or *Kyrios* (owner), *Basil* (royal or king); German: *Bern* (bear) or *Bernard* (Bold as a Bear); Hebrew: *Baal* (Master or Lord); Russian: *Boyar* (nobleman); Scottish: *Laird* (Lord); Turkish: *khan* (ruler). A word in a language that others might easily understand should probably be avoided. So it would be best to avoid some common Western European languages.

Another alternative is to choose a normal name but one that has an appropriate authoritative meaning: Aaron (lofty, high), Andrew (manly), Arnold (strong), Barret (mighty as a bear), Basil (kingly), Boris (a fighter), Conal (high and mighty), Cyril (Lord), Duke (leader), Earl (nobleman), Fergus (best choice, strong man), Grant (great), Hiram (most noble), Igor (hero), Rex (King), etc. Some Masters may choose an anagram of Master such as Tamers, Stream,[41] Semtar; or of Sir (Ris).

In some cases, even the slave is given a new name, one that reflects his status as a submissive. For example, *doulos* (Greek), *ebed* (Hebrew), or as my current Master calls me (the) thrall (Old English for slave).[42]

---

[41] Especially appropriate for a watersports Master.
[42] See Chapter 43. Maintaining a Master/Slave Relationship.

Chapter 7

Slave Speech or Slave-Speak

The first rule of slave speech is that when communicating to the Master, every utterance, no matter how short, should contain the word "sir," and when beginning and/or ending with that word, it should be emphasized "Sir!" In some cases, the still more formal or intense, "Master" may be more appropriate. When using Sir or Master within an utterance, the title does not need to be emphasized, as in, "What does Sir wish this slave to do?" To allow this formal speech pattern to be compromised by vanilla speech is a major loss of a tool to maintain a strong M/s relationship.

When accompanying one's Master in public, it is the general rule that the slave remains silent unless or until the Master allows the slave to say something. When this happens, the slave should give only the minimum response. In short, he does not offer any unsolicited information. In this restraint on talking it is important for the slave to distinguish between yes/no questions and wh- questions, which require more of a verbal response. This limiting of a slave's speech may be especially important in first meeting a potential Master, as might happen in a leather bar.

First, the potential slave should not approach the potential Master unless the Master signals him to approach. Of course, this sometimes requires the slave to creatively bump into the Master, followed by an obvious humbling apology; otherwise, if the slave is cruising and sees a Master he is interested in and the Master is staring at the slave, the slave should nod his head to indicate such an interest and then wait for any further response from the Master.

Once the Master either approaches the slave or signals for the slave to approach him, the dialog, which should be initiated by the Master, not the slave, might go something like this:

Master: "Good evening."

"Good evening, Sir!" (Do not be so informal as to say "Hello" unless the Master uses such an informal greeting.)

"I see you're wearing a collar." [43]

"Yes, Sir!"

"Are you from around here?"

"Yes (or No), Sir!"

(If no) "Where are you from?"

"From X, Sir!" Commonly one would start with "I am …" but a slave tries to avoid personal reference to himself, so the slave tries to either avoid that pronoun or replaces it with the impersonal "This slave or this boy." [44]

The slave here has given only the necessary information. This, plus the repeated "Sir!" should automatically single the slave out as a submissive and one who is clearly well disciplined in his speech protocol. Remember, the slave stands tall for this, with shoulders back, so as not to be thought of as timid, since the limited responses may be mistaken for shyness.

"What's your name, boy?"

"X, Sir!"

"What are you looking for, boy?"

"To serve a Master to the best of this slave's ability, Sir!"

From this point on, the negotiations would begin, and without being too talkative, the slave has the right and responsibility to ask any question he believes is necessary to ensure the potential Master is safe to submit to.

In a clear Master/slave encounter, to have volunteered too much unsolicited information is technically an offense, and the Master has every right, even an obligation, to respond with something like, "That's more information than I asked for, boy. If I wanted to know that, I would have asked it."

"Yes, Sir! This slave's mistake, Sir! This slave apologizes. Please pardon him, Sir!"

---

[43] See Chapter 17. Slave Collars.
[44] See Chapter 7. Slave Speech.

Sometimes, however, a simple yes/no question cannot or should not be answered with a yes or no. For example, I met a hot Dom who, once it became obvious to him that I was assuming the status of a submissive, suddenly and forcefully grabbed the back of my neck, which sent a shudder down my body. This was less from the suddenness or forcefulness than from the excitement of his taking charge of me. The Dom clearly did not know this, and the conversation went like this, "Do I make you nervous?"

"Sir! This slave believes (~~I believe~~) Sir (~~you~~) should answer that. Does this slave (~~he~~) have any need to be nervous or frightened, Sir?"

After a minute's delay, I got back, "No. I respect any limits you tell me you have."

"In that case, Sir! [45] hand reassuring."

We ended up having really good power-exchange sex.

Note that my complete answer above, although much wordier than a simple yes/no, gave the Dom (the questioner) the minimum information he asked for, while also telling him that I did need to feel safe in any play. It also told him that I was truly willing to be his submissive. This was reinforced with every utterance beginning and/or ending in Sir! This is a speech habit that every slave should condition himself to use whenever he is with his Master. Not to do so shows mindlessness, laziness, and disrespect. It also means one is falling back into the offensive vanilla mind-set.

There are two reasons for a slave to minimize his verbalization. First, it shows that the slave is not trying to impose information on the Master. Second, that slave is not a boringly chatty type. My first Master would say, "To convince anyone you're a bore, keep talking; and any slave who is a bore is unworthy of a Master." Such chattiness is a punishable offense for any sub or slave who dominates a conversation, weather in the presence of his Master or not, as it betrays his slave status. The default condition of a slave is one of silence.

Many Masters expect their slaves in public to learn to communicate with each other nonverbally. This is especially so if the two are in a space within the scene. This communication is usually achieved through hand and/or finger gestures. For example, a Master who, for whatever reason, does not wish to verbally tell his slave to get him a drink may signal the

---

[45] See Chapter 7. Slave Speech.

slave by a subtle placing of his hand on his neck. The slave could also use this sign to ask the Master if he (the slave) could have a drink. The Master subtly running an open or closed hand down his chest could mean sit down, or running it up the chest could signal stand up. The slave making the same gesture would be a request to sit down or stand up. Some Masters prefer to use certain finger signals, which can almost be a complicated as sign language.

There are several benefits to this nonverbal communication. First, requiring a slave to learn to use such gestures as a replacement for normal verbal communication reinforces the slave's sense of being under the Master's control and the Master's sense of having control of the slave. Second, in a non-Scene situation where verbal "commands" may attract too much attention from outsiders, this silent communication allows for the Master/slave mind-set to remain in force, rather than having to go vanilla for a shorter or longer time. Third, in that this is a private or secret language known only to the Master and slave, it puts them both in a world all their own, which can only intensify the bond between them. Fourth, in a sense, it trains the slave to limit his "speaking" to a minimum as is proper to all slaves. Finally, it forces the slave to keep his full attention on his Master, especially his shoulders and hands, in case he should miss a signal.

The rule for any gesture is that it should be noticeable to the Master and slave but unnoticeable to all others. This might include not being noticeable even in a Scene situation, so it seems as if the Master and slave are reading each other's minds. This will certain be the envy of those around them.

Some Masters may allow their slaves to open a dialog with a "Sir! May this slave ask a question?" Sometimes a slave must anticipate the need of his Master with "Sir! Do you wish this slave to X?" However, the slave must always remember that he is best if unseen and unheard, unless to otherwise please his Master. Of course, if the slave believes that he should add a limited amount of extra information to either a yes/no or wh- question, he might say, "Sir, may I add to this?" However, any such permission to do so should be limited, so as not to be abused.

Except for the most minimal information, and then only when directly asked, a slave does not speak about his Master without permission from his Master. This also applies to a former Master, unless the slave feels that such a Master has been abusive and other slaves or Masters should be given a warning about such abusiveness.

Of course, if a slave is speaking to another slave without a Master present, the two can be more familiar (informal, relaxed) with one another, but they are still responsible for reminding one another (reinforcing among themselves) that they are slaves by always addressing each other as "slave X." Likewise, if two Masters are speaking to one another, they may do so with more informality. The greatest amount of formality comes in a mixed Master/slave situation. If a Master is present, then the slaves speak to each other only minimally; and of course, this starts with the permission of the slaves to speak in the first place. The more formal manner, as stated above, comprises minimizing speech to the yes/no or minimal wh-question/answer level, even between slaves.

It should not be forgotten that even in private, there may be limits placed on the talkativeness of a slave, especially during a scene. While good communication between players is important, all but the minimum talking can ruin the scene, even in vanilla sex.

Naturally, any of the above rules will need to be relaxed if and when the Master allows the slave to go out of slave mode, as would be necessary outside of a power/authority-exchanging environment.

One good training rule for a slave is that before he speaks even to his Master he should silently count one-two-three-four-five. This will help to keep him in slave awareness as well as saving him on many occasions from a punishable misspeak. The one exception is when the slave is expected to instantly reply to his Master with a, "Yes! Sir!" or "No! Sir!"

Finally, whenever a slave is talking to or just listening to his Master, his head should always be turned toward the Master as a sign of respectful devotion.

Returning to the use of pronouns, if the depersonalization of the slave by replacing "I" with "this slave" is self-humbling, even more so is the purely general or unspecified "the slave('s)." While this may seem extreme, the fact is that training oneself to absolutely minimize the normal use of personal pronouns is a major way to reduce normal self-absorbtion. However, this requires a great deal of practice and self-discipline and a great deal of reinforcement from the Master.

Obviously, this dropping of *I, me, my, myself,* and *mine* is going to be especially difficult in a vanilla setting, but with a lot of practice, it can be done with a moderate amount of success. In place of "I need xxx," "This sub/slave needs xxx" will do in the Scene, but outside the Scene, one might try "Is it possible to have that?" In a restaurant, instead of saying to the waiter, "I would like xxx," the sub could just go with, "How about xxxx?" or even just, "Xxx, please." The sub in a store trying to buy a shirt could avoid "I'm looking for xxx" with "What do you have in a xxx?" A motivated sub/slave's creativity should never be underappreciated, and while this kind of self-monitoring of speech may seem a real hassle at first, many slaves may eventually become so skilled at it that they will actually prize their ability.

Should any Master be serious about his slave surrendering his right to use the self-reinforcing personal pronoun references, that Master will need to be a model for the slave. This means that he too should train himself, or better the two train each other, to avoid such pronoun usage. For example, instead of the Master saying, "I want you to polish my boots," which has very little M/s flavor to it, he could say, "Boy (or slave), you need to polish your Master's boots," or even more intense depersonalizing would be, "Slave, this Master's boots need polishing." In that instance, the slave is gloriously reminded of their respective positions. One advantage to such mutual verbal training will be to intensify any bond the two share.

In this process of verbal depersonalizing, one should still remember that the slave continues to be a human being and must never be treated as less. Should this be forgotten, the slave should tell his Master to "go to hell" and leave to find a Master who understands the difference between fantasy and reality.

After the restrictions on the first-person pronoun, the next restrictions might be on the second-person pronoun (you, your). When speaking to one's Master or any familiar Master, the slave should try not to treat him as he would an ordinary person. The slave might say to a family member, coworker, or even the Master in the non-kinky public environment, "What would you like?" "How was your day?" "Did you like the show?" "You need to buy more rope." However, to say something similar to that to the Master, at least in private, is to make no attempt to single him out as someone special, and especially to the slave. Therefore, on the slave's own initiative or as a requirement of the Master, the slave may drop all these you/your words and replace them with Sir('s) or the Master('s). With this in mind, the slave might say, "What would Sir/the Master like?" "How was Sir's/the Master's day?" "Did Sir/the Master like the show?" "Sir! The Master needs to buy more rope."

Again, if this is the Master's requirement, he should be the model with, "The slave's mother called," or "Does the slave have any suggestion as to what the Master and the slave might do this weekend?"[46] When the Master asks a question like this, the slave has two proper choices. He can say "No, Sir!" since ultimately it is the Master's right to plan for the weekend, and the slave's response properly reflects this fact. On the other hand, if the slave really does have a suggestion and really does want the Master to consider it, the slave can say, "Is Sir ordering the slave to offer a suggestion, Sir?" Here, the slave has made it clear that he accepts the fact that he has no ultimate right to a suggestion and would not give one unless ordered to do so by the Master. If the Master says, "That is an order," then the slave is free to (obligated to) give a suggestion.

In every one of these sentences, the slave is not allowed to forget he is a slave for even a moment, and the Master is not allowed to forget that he is a Master. Just such forgetting is a common occurrence in long-term M/s relationships, and this pronoun restriction can be a powerful tool to reduce that forgetting or at least hold it off for some time.

The avoidance of the personal pronoun may also help communicate to the Master that the slave would be open to doing something, but to say, "Sir! I would like to go to a movie tonight" might receive from the Master, "I don't care what you want." However, if the slave phrases it as, "Sir! This slave was wondering whether or not Sir would like to go to a movie tonight?" the Master obviously knows that this means the slave would like to go, but he has phrased it with the focus not on himself, but on the Master. Chances are better now that the Master will say yes.

For some Masters, the constant use of the word *slave* in these contexts might seem too impersonal or too harsh, in which case *you/your* would be replaced with "the boy" or even the slave's slave name, both of which are

---

[46] Note that here even the first person plural (we) has been replaced by "the Master and the slave."

By extension this could go for "us/our."

still in the third person; thus "Xxxx needs to polish his Master's boots." Likewise, the slave could soften his speech with "X Sir" or "Master X."

This kind of verbal reconditioning is not going to happen quickly and may never become perfect, because every time the slave and the Master go out into the non-slave world, they are going to have to revert to the normal pronoun usage when in a vanilla conversation with others or simply within earshot of others; thus, the Master (and slave) may decide that it takes too much effort and stay with or revert back to normal usage altogether.

However, if the two decide, at least, to try to adopt this unique and empowering Master/slave speech, and this is a joint project, one way to do this would be that each time the slave makes a mistake the Master might face the slave with an expression suggesting the slave's utterance is incomprehensible. The same process would be used in the reverse. On the other hand, the receiver of the utterance could simply repeat the utterance only in the proper manner. Since this requires both parties to assist (reinforce) one another, any mistakes should not come under the category of a punishable offense, unless the slave is not showing an honest effort.

Because going from the use of personal pronouns to third-person nouns is extremely stressful if tried all at once, it is probably best to do it gradually. A certain number of first-person pronouns could be tolerated each day, but for every three after that, some mild punishment can be required.[47] Each week, the number of tolerated uses can be reduced until none are acceptable and all references are in the third person.

Even if this pronoun reduction is not used at home all the time, it should at least be used when the slave is trying to apologize to the Master by showing greater-than-usual deference, as in "This slave (I) apologizes to Sir (even better "to his Master") and begs for his Master's (your) pardon."[48] Also, remember that one of the most often-used phrases by a slave should be "Thank you, Sir!" Therefore, if "you" is one of the pronouns to be

---

[47] With the slave taking the punishment for the Master's misuse of the pronouns. See Chapter 23. Punishment.

[48] Remember, *pardon* is a better word than *forgive* for a slave to use, as it has more of a dominance quality to it.

avoided, a substitute must be found such as "This slave thanks the Sir/ Master" or in the reverse, "The Master thanks the slave."

Actually, such speech discipline is not only for Masters and slaves but for any spiritual discipline that emphasizes letting go of one's ego. It is a fairly well known that in ordinary conversation, a speaker spends more time with references to him- or herself than to any other person or thing. This only serves to reinforce the sense of selfhood or how important "I" is. The Master and the slave need to keep in mind that there is nothing inherently natural about an M/s relationship, and one way to constantly reinforce that relationship is to learn to use unnatural or Master/slave jargon.

Chapter 8

Slave Gaze

Some Masters insist that their slave show them deference by not looking directly at the face of the Master, but keep their gaze lowered. This can be anywhere from the chin to the chest of the Master, with the Master's feet as the target only during punishment. Other Masters only require the slave to seemingly lower his gaze in the presence of that Master in such a fashion that while the slave's face is angled just enough downward that it appears he is looking downward, in fact, his eyes are actually able to look up to check the countenance of the Master. Still other Masters require the slave to look directly at the Master's face as a sign of total attention to the Master's words. However, when a slave is with his own Master, he should not look at another Master directly in the face unless given permission to do so by his own Master, as if and when the slave is allowed to shake the hand of that other Master.[49]

The lowered gaze of a slave should never be misinterpreted as shyness or fear. To avoid this mistake, the slave should always stand as erect as possible, head held high and hands at his side or behind his back. Such a posture implies self-discipline and the courage to be a proud slave. Self-discipline, in fact, is essential if a slave intends to keep a Master; however, this self-discipline should not be too bold, least the Master thinks it is in competition with his own self-discipline.

---

[49] See Chapter 9. Hand Shaking and Greeting.

Chapter 9

Handshaking and Other Greetings

The Master/slave handshaking ritual is something to be taken very seriously. If two Masters meet, the standard non-leather handshaking is appropriate, but when it comes to a slave greeting a Master who is not his own, the issue becomes more ritualized. In one tradition, a slave never shakes the hand of another Master; instead, from a standing position and with his feet together, he bows his head momentarily. In another tradition, the slave may shake the hand of another Master only after a verbal or head-nodding permission from his own Master. The slave, however, should first wipe his hand on his clothing, assuming he is wearing some, to signal that he would never offer a possibly soiled hand to any Master. Some Masters will give a slave an automatic permission to shake the hand of another Master who both the slave and his Master are familiar with, but not with an unfamiliar Master. In extremely liberal situations, a Master may allow a slave to accept a normal (vanilla) greeting, as long as the Master has been greeted first.

There is also the issue of how two slaves should greet one another. In a stricture tradition, the slave from a relaxed (two feet apart) standing position, simply nods to the other slave if one or both is in the presence of one or both of their Masters. In a more relaxed tradition, two slaves with the permission of both their Masters may shake each other's hand without first hand wiping, as the two slaves are equals.

Also, when a slave communicates with another slave, the two should always address one another as "slave Bob, slave John," etc. If both slaves are from the same household, this may be relaxed. If one or both slaves are training alphas, the proper address would be "alpha slave x."[50] Moreover, if only one of the slaves is recognized by both Masters as a training alpha slave, the nonalpha should wipe his hand. A gamma (slave in training) regards an alpha (training) slave as a lesser Master and so greets him with an "Alpha Sir" or just "Sir."

This protocol is a little different for a slave looking for a Master. Upon meeting a Dom or Master, even if he is not interested in the person as a potential Master, the slave still shows deference by having one hand behind his back, as any slave would, and only extending the other hand to greet the Dom or Master.

Finally, in some traditions, the slave should not smile at another Master, as this suggests too much familiarity. Some Masters even feel that during a conversation with anyone other than the Master and slave, the slave should totally avoid laughing at something that is amusing. However, if the slave must offer some polite response, a subtle smile is generally acceptable.

---

[50] See 48. Alpha Slave.

Chapter 10

Standing Positions, Sitting Down, and Walking

There are generally four different slave standing positions: (1) legs and feet together, hands at the sides; (2) legs spread, hands at the sides; (3) legs together, hands behind back; and (4) legs spread, hands behind back. The head may or may not be slightly bowed in these unless the slave is required to look more directly at someone speaking to him. The slave's eyes should not normally be floor gazing. This is only appropriate if the slave has done something seriously wrong and is being verbally shouted at by his Master. This is assuming his Master does not demand he look directly at him.[51]

When a familiar or unfamiliar Master approaches a slave, that slave ought to immediately assume the most formal standing slave posture, which is number one. This posture (at attention) is taken when first greeting a Master, assuming a kneeling position is not required. It is rarely held for long, except as a form of punishment. Number two is a formal position mostly assumed in a non-leather situation where number one would result in too much attention from others. Number three is a semiformal position, which the slave would take immediately after number one, unless his Master requires him to remain in number one. Number four is also called "parade rest" or "at ease," and is taken when the most relaxed position is allowed. This will be the standing position the slave most commonly takes when alongside his Master.

---

[51] See Chapter 8. Slave Gaze.

If communications between a slave and a Master are for some reason being impeded by the slave being in any of the above slave positions, he may, under certain circumstances, request leaving the slave mode to facilitate further communications.

Along with the proper standing protocol is the walking one. Under most circumstances, the slave walks by the Master's side (shoulder or sole walking) or just behind to one side (heel walking). In the first case, the Master is always able to see and take hold of the slave. In the second, he is made to understand that the Master leads, the slave follows. Only under rare circumstances is the slave in front of the Master (toe walking). While some Masters wish their slaves to walk with their hands behind them, this can be problematic. No one walking is ever totally immune from an accidental tripping that sends the body forward and downward to the ground. When this happens, instinct causes one's hands to try to cushion the fall, to protect the head from damage. If a slave has his hands behind him, he is more likely to suffer harm. For this reason, while in motion, the slave's arms and hands are best by his side in a natural walking position; however, every time the Master stops, the slave's arms and hands should go behind him until the Master is again in motion.

In the United States, a slave most often will walk on the Master's right. This is common because the driver (the one in charge of the vehicle) sits on the left while the passenger is on the right.[52] However, a left-handed Master may prefer his slave to walk on the left side, as it is most likely that the Master will command the slave with that dominant hand.

Naturally, there are reasons for modifying this walking procedure, such as when the Master is really required to lead the way or if a walk space is too narrow for walking abreast. In this latter case, it is up to the Master to decide how the slave should proceed. Also, when approaching a closed door, it is the slave's responsibility to open that door for his Master, which is one of the few times he will move in front of his Master.[53]

There is one more major stance a sub or slave my find himself in—the anal-genital inspection one. The naked slave stands with his legs apart, bent over at the waist with knees slightly bent for balance, his hands holding

---

[52] In a country that drives on the left, the opposite may be the case.

[53] In a bar, a Master may be behind a slave he is literally pushing toward the door.

on to his ankles or as far down the legs as possible, and his head down so he can see between his legs. This position allows his Dominant to visually see the slave's anus and genitals and to inspect them with fingers and/or tongue. This position is not recommended for more than a short time, as it is easy, especially for an older sub, to lose his balance.

When it comes to the issue of the Master and slave sitting, each Master has his own preference. Some Masters believe the slave should always stand until the Master sits. Other Masters do not want the slave's head higher than that of the Master, so the slave is expected to sit down first. If the Master must sit first, then the higher head of the slave can be compensated for by the slave remaining in the slave stance (arms behind the back) until his Master signals permission for him to sit. This same compensation can apply whenever the slave approaches a seated Master. Naturally, the relative height of the Master and slave may affect the situation, especially if the Master is shorter than the slave.

While some Masters only tolerate slaves shorter than themselves, I have known several Master/slave relationships in which the Master is much shorter than the slave. In one case, the slave sought out a shorter Master, so as to experience even greater (empowered) humiliation by serving him. The point to this is that being a Master or slave is state of mind, not of height. In theory, a dwarf could be the Master of a full-sized adult slave, although that could have obvious practical problems.

One rigid rule is that a slave should never sit in a chair with arms if the Master is in an armless chair. Moreover, if there is a difference in the height of the back of the chair, the Master sits in the higher-backed one unless the lower-backed one is more comfortable. Also, out of respect for all Masters, no slave should be sitting in a chair if this leaves another Master standing. Some Masters require that the slave sits only on a backless chair (stool) or slave seat during home dining, assuming he is not required to sit on the floor to eat.[54] Since most outside facilities do not provide such backless seats, the slave generally sits on a regular chair in that situation. [55]

In those cases where a slave is allowed to sit on a chair, couch, or stool, he should sit with his back straight, never slouching, and never with his

---

[54] Most Masters only use this as a punishment.
[55] See Chapter 12. Public and Private Eating Behavior.

legs or even ankles crossed. For a slave to have his legs crossed or one leg (the calf) crossing another (the thigh) means the slave's crotch is shielded from his Master's view, which is the equivalent of saying *I am not available to Sir.* Instead, the slave's feet should be firmly placed on the floor with his legs spread apart, and his hands should be palms down on his thighs or knees, never placed together in his lap, which again hides his crotch from his Master's view.[56]

A slave trying to recondition himself not to cross his legs can be a particularly difficult habit to break. For this reason, when a slave is caught doing so, some Masters will require the slave to wear a leg-spreader bar anywhere from two to four hours, and after a few weeks, this will help to break the offending habit.

This spreader is sometimes used as a toy, as when a Master wants the slave's legs spread for rimming, fucking, etc. However, as long as it is used for this habit-breaking purpose, the spreader should not be used as a sex toy. Instead, if the Master wants a slave's legs spread for sex, the ankles can spread in some other fashion. Once the ankle-cross habit is broken, the spreader can go back to being used as a sex toy.

To avoid making any of the above sitting mistakes, some slaves, taking no chances, prefer to just sit on the floor where they can cross ankles and legs (Indian style); in that fashion, the crotch is fully exposed to the Master's view as long as the hands are kept on the thighs.

There is another advantage to such floor sitting. Many Masters insist that each time they rise from a chair, the slave should also rise, but most Masters exempt a slave who is sitting on the floor from this because by being on the floor, the sub is showing complete deference toward his Master, and popping up from that position each time a Master gets up should be unnecessary overkill and in a non-kink environment draw unnecessary attention.

A slave may be permitted to sit on the floor/ground cross-legged in almost any social situation that does not require him to sit on a chair. If a Master and slave are at a non-kink social event and they still want to keep some degree of Master/slave protocol, the Master may respond to

---

[56] See Chapter 11. Kneeling Procedures.

any question as to why the slave is sitting on the floor with, "He likes it on the floor."

When sitting in a restaurant, the slave will sit in accordance with the wishes of his Master, with the only rule being that if the two are in the company of others, no other person should sit between them.[57]

Naturally, as mentioned before, these rules mostly apply to a sitting situation, where such rules are understood and not among the general public where the Master/slave relationship might be seen in a negative light. Also, none of these rules apply to a slave who is temporarily a free agent unless the slave himself chooses to voluntarily follow them which might be important in finding a new Master and/or reducing Slave Identity Drift."[58] If upon meeting a potential new Master, the slave is too relaxed in his behavior it could result in either turning the Master off or attracting a Master of inferior quality.

Also, when with a Master a slave does not stand or sit with his arms crossed unless the Master, for some reason, permits such crossing the arms as when it is obviously cold outside. Otherwise, such a crossing implies either a closing off of the body to the Master and/or is taken as a sign of anger toward him. The same may or may not apply to hands, since that means the arms are across the chest. As an open hand is a sign of openness or surrender, some Masters feel that slaves should not lock the fingers of their hands together, but when not in use, they should be kept palms down on the slave's thighs. Other Masters feel that if the slave is sitting at a table and his hands are on the slave's thighs, those hands are out of the view of the Master and too close to the slave's crotch which, he should not be tempted to touch without the Master's permission.

---

[57] See 12. Public and Private Eating Behavior.
[58] See 27. Slave Identity Drift.

Chapter 11

Kneeling Procedures

A slave kneels before his Master or another Master (1) as the ultimate respectful greeting; (2) as a sign of complete submission to his own or a potentially new Master; or (3) in front of his own Master in acknowledgment that he has done something wrong (violated protocol) and wishes to apologize and seek pardon for it.[59]

Kneeling as a supreme sign of formal submissiveness should never be done causally. It is always to be treated with great respect by both a Dom/Master and a sub/slave. For this reason, it is done only in an environment that recognizes the full meaning and value of the act. Thus, it should be confined to either a private M/s situation or where like-minded people are gathered, such as a play party or in a real leather bar. I say *real* because most of the patrons in most so-called leather bars, even most of those wearing leather, are actually into vanilla and will be more amused by such a display of submission than appreciative of it. Even in a genuine kink environment, a sub or slave does not walk up to an unknown Dom or Master and, without permission, kneel before him. This is regarded as the sub/slave imposing his submissiveness on the Dom or Master. It is called bottom disease, and it is a violation of sub/slave protocol.

As far as the mechanics of kneeling, there are eight major kneeling positions.

---

[59] This is the minimum non-erotic discipline (punishment) a slave accepts.

(1)   The formal half-kneeling in which the slave will be down only on one knee with the butt raised so as not to rest on that leg (calf). This first position is taken for a very short time, such as when greeting a Master, after which the slave will probably be expected to stand. If the slave is going to be in a half-kneeling position for a longer period, he will probably be allowed to assume the more comfortable position two.

(2)   The informal half-kneeling in which the slave's butt is resting on his calf.

(3)   The formal full kneeling, in which the slave with legs together will be down on both knees, but with the butt not resting on the calves (kneeling high). Both Masters and slaves regard this as a favorite position, for it generally puts the slave's face at the same height as the Master's crotch.

(4)   The informal full kneeling is with legs together and the butt resting on both the calves (kneeling low). This is not recommended for long periods, as it can cut off circulation in the legs. Positions three and four are most often assumed when kneeling before one's Master while receiving orders or being reprimanded.

(5)   This is the same as three except with the legs comfortably apart. Thus, it is assumed if the kneeling is for a longer period.

(6)   The same as four except with the legs comfortably apart. Thus, it is assumed if the kneeling is for a longer period.
      In cases one to four, the hands will be kept behind the back. In five and six, the hands will be either on the sides of the legs or resting on the thighs.[60] Five and six, which are also the most natural way of kneeling, call the least attention to the kneeler and are mostly used in social settings, where a compromise may be required. For some Masters, all of the above kneeling positions (1–6) require that the legs be kept apart, not together, so that the Master always has a view of the slave's crotch.[61]

---

[60]   Position six is traditional Japanese style.
[61]   See Chapter 10. Standing, Sitting Down, Walking.

(7) The last major kneeling position is with the palms of the hands pressed against the ground. This is the "on all fours" position.[62] This is mainly used when the slave needs to deeply humble himself animal-like to apologize to the Master and/or receive a blow to his buttocks. The Master needs to be careful in this punishment situation, since the slave's testicles are completely exposed (unprotected) and could be accidentally hit.

(8) A variation of the all-fours protocol position will have the calves tucked under the butt; and the forehead may even be pressed against the ground. This is the standard "kowtow position" and again is a sign of the slave's humble remorse for some serious wrongdoing. This position may be punishment in itself if the slave is required to remain in it for long.

A final reason for a slave to be in the all-fours position is for Master adoration or worship. This will usually start with standard kissing and/ or licking the feet or boots of the Master but goes beyond simple foot fetish action by a repeated kowtowing. This would mostly be done by a slave who does not have some spiritual practice separate from his Master and so treats his Master as a higher power. For those slaves who do relate to a higher spiritual something outside the Master, any deification of the Master would be inappropriate.

It must be emphasized that kneeling in any position for any great length of time is not natural to the body and, if overdone, can lead to stress on the knees, legs, butt, back, and neck, so the responsible Master does not allow the slave to spend more than a few minutes in any of the above positions without allowing for periodic standing. However, kneeling is so much a part of a slave's protocol that he should never go a day without finding a reason to do it on his own if his Master has not decided upon one. Starting and ending each day are ideal times for a slave to kneel before his Master with a "Good morning, Sir! It is this slave's deepest wish that today go well for his Master;" and/or "Good night, Sir! I hope that this slave has satisfactorily served his Master this day."

---

[62] It is called a protocol position to distinguish it from the same position used in doggy style intercourse.

Chapter 12

Public and Private Eating Behavior

As mentioned above, when sitting in a restaurant, the slave will sit in accordance with the wishes of his Master, with the only absolute rule being that if the two are in the company of others, no other person should sit between them. Since a restaurant is such a public place, most Masters do not wish to call attention to themselves or their slaves by requiring a protocol that would make them both stand out too much, but this does not mean that subtle protocol cannot or should not be observed. For an example of such protocol, I will use that required by one Master I knew.

    (1)   The slave will walk in front of the Master to open and/or hold open the door.

    (2)   The slave will then return to the dominant-hand side of the Master.

    (3)   If the two are to sit at a counter or free-standing table, the Master will sit first, nod to the slave to sit, again next to his dominant side. If the Master and slave are sitting at a table or booth, one side of which is against a wall, and they are sitting opposite one another, then the Master should sit on the side that leaves his dominant hand on the outside versus on the wall side. The slave then sits on the opposite side. An alternative to this is the slave side is that which allows the slave's non-dominant (noneating) hand near the wall, so that that hand can be subtly held behind his back while eating. The reason for this hand position is that, unlike at a free-standing table, the Master has no immediate

58

ability to seize the slave by the upper arm (a sign of control); therefore, as a countersign of dominance, the slave is to keep his noneating hand behind his back, as if he were in a standing and waiting position. If this hand position would cause more attention to the Master and slave than the Master wishes, as would be the case if the booth is open at both ends, the Master may simply tell the slave to keep that hand on the seat.

Before going any further, it must be mentioned that just because a Master takes a slave to a restaurant does not automatically mean the slave has a right to eat there. Therefore, the Master must notify the slave that this right is being offered him.

(4)   The slave will not touch the menu until the Master does.

(5)   The Master will respond to a waiter's question about any water or other drinks.

(6)   The slave will read the menu in silence.

(7)   The Master will choose his meal and inform the slave of that choice. The slave will take that choice into consideration when choosing his own meal since (a) a slave may not order a larger meal than a Master without special permission, and (b) he may not order something that would be offensive to the Master without special permission, unless there was a health reason for doing so. For example, if the Master is a vegetarian, the slave should not order meat.

(8)   Since the Master will (or should) know if the slave has any significant issues with certain kinds of food, he will not expect the slave to order anything problematic, but beyond that, the slave will, "upon being asked," tell the Master of his choice(s). Preferably, he will give the Master more than one choice.

(9)   The Master will either automatically accept the one choice or choose one of the alternatives. I have yet to meet a Master who does not allow his slave to choose what he wishes to eat or not eat, since this makes for a control-freak Master. However, unless given previous permission, a slave should not automatically assume he has the full freedom to order his food without running it by the Master. A simple, "Sir! I (or 'this slave,' said quietly) would like to have X," should be sufficient to satisfy any slave protocol.

(10) Either the Master will do the ordering for both himself and the slave or, as not to call too much attention to them, the slave will be allowed to tell the waiter what he wishes to order.

(11) The slave will never order an alcoholic beverage himself. The Master will order this for him only after the Master has asked the slave if he would like one. The slave may never ask the Master to have one.

(12) The slave will not pick up cutlery before the Master does.

(13) The slave will eat in silence unless the Master prefers otherwise.

(14) If the slave has not finished eating before the Master does, the slave will stop as soon as the Master stops.

(15) The issue of paying this, or any bill, will be decided within the parameters of the contract.

(16) The slave may not waste any food that is paid for by his Master. It shows a lack of self-discipline.

These rules will have to be modified for a female slave of a male Master, as it would be regarded as socially inappropriate for a woman to wait for a male to sit down or for her to have to get up each time he got up.

Much of the restaurant protocol also applies at home. If the slave has prepared a meal for the Master—and presumably for himself—he serves the Master first and waits for the Master to signal that he may serve himself. The slave sits near the dominant hand of the Master; he does not eat more than the Master; he does not continue eating after the Master has finished; he does not speak during the meal without permission; and he remains seated until the Master arises or gives the slave permission to stand up. These rules will need to be modified at home if the slave is expected to eat sitting on the floor.

Chapter 13

Restroom Use

That a slave should have to ask permission to use the restroom may seem a good example of a Master who is an absolute control freak, but this need not be the case. Such asking is not really about the right to urinate or defecate; this would actually be carrying control of the slave to an abusive degree, and a "good Master is not a control freak." Instead, it is a humble way of letting the Master know that the slave has an immediate need to leave the Master's side, nothing more. This author has never heard of a Master refusing that right.[63]

The free use of the restroom should not be just a matter when away from home. Every morning, the slave might automatically ask for that day to use the bathroom without necessarily asking the Master each time the slave needed to do so. Likewise, each night before the Master goes to bed, the slave might ask for the right to use the bathroom if necessary, so he does not have to wake the Master up for permission. If the slave forgets to ask for this nighttime permission, he has a choice: he can wake the Master to ask for permission and thereby incur the Master's displeasure at being woken up, or he can take nature's call and absolutely should confess to his Master his forgetting to ask in advance. Either way, the slave should ask to receive his due punishment. If he is not punished, it will soon corrupt his slavery.

---

[63] What this author has heard of is that one Master insisted that the slave rather than using the toilet seat, he had to lift it up and sit on the porcelain rim.

While on the issue of the restroom, it should be mentioned that at home, some Masters will allow a slave to shut the bathroom door while inside, and other Masters regard this as creating a barrier between the slave and Master.

Chapter 14

Slave Wear I, Nudity

In many cultures in which there has been legal slavery, it was always assumed that the slaves dressed less well than their Masters; in fact, in some such cultures, free persons were always dressed, at least covering their genitals, while slaves were required to be nude like some less-than-human animal. This is one reason why a Master should never undress, or at least expose his genitals, to a slave before the slave has undressed or exposed his to the Master.

Humiliating nudity is very much a part of most Master/slave traditions, and in many M/s households, the slave is expected to be completely nude, weather permitting. If such total nudity is impractical, then the standard compromised rule is that the slave never wears more clothes, preferably always fewer clothes, than the Master.

When clothes are permitted, a few things can be taken into consideration, starting with underwear. In earlier times, it was a rule that higher-ranking people either wore underwear or wore more of it than lower-ranking people. This has been retained in some M/s tradition, wherein slaves should not wear underwear, especially underpants. This is because they believe the slave's butt and cock should always be as accessible as is practically possible to his Master's touch or more, and so the slave should not wear anything that would be contrary to this.

Because social law requires everyone to keep their private areas covered in public, the slave must wear pants while outside the home, but underwear is not required, and by requiring the slave to be nude under his street pants, he is reminded that he is a slave throughout the day.

On the other hand, some Masters require the wearing of underwear or a jock strap for one or more of the following reasons: (a) for the practical purpose that it holds in any erection of the slave that might occur at an inappropriate time; (b) to prevent any precum stain from becoming obvious on the slave's pants; (c) because many Masters find the look of underwear or the jock strap erotically arousing when the slave's pants are taken off; (d) the jock may preserve the visual and olfactory signs of the slave's urine and precum, which is pleasing to some Masters; and (d) the jock, especially soiled one, can be used as a convenient gag for the slave.[64] Also, there is the situation where it is not the Master who has a particular fetish for underwear but the slave, and the sensible Master should be willing to accept and take advantage of this.

There is one other less-common so-called undergarment, but actually more of a wearable toy, the butt-plug harness. Some Masters insist that whenever the slave is at his home, the slave wears one, except during sleep. This is the Master's way of forcing his slave to feel fucked even when the real thing isn't up his asshole. A few Masters actually require their slaves to wear the plug under their outside clothes whenever they are together.

It should be a general rule that whatever outside or street clothes a slave wears, these should not automatically be acceptable to wear in the Master's home. If full or partial nudity is not required, obvious evidence of his non-slave outside life should be removed and replaced with something that more or less defines the slave as a slave.

It is important to understand that a slave's physical nudity is more than the sexual exposure of not wearing clothes; it symbolizes that the slave must be naked psychologically. Clothes are a kind of armor that hides and protects us from others, and a slave has volunteered to be vulnerable to his Master's authority, power, will, and desires. This clothing as armor is most obvious in any heavy leather bar.

Caution: remember, a naked or genital-showing slave may be visible to neighbors through a window, and one does not usually want a naked slave to answer the door unless it is to drive away really obnoxious individuals. For this reason, it may be practical for the Master to answer the door while the slave retreats into another room.

---

[64] Some Masters reserve the leather jock for themselves and the cloth for the slave.

Chapter 15

Slave Wear II

As mentioned above (in "Slave Wear I"), a slave should never show less skin than his Master; therefore, when it comes to shirts and pants, a slave should never wear long-sleeved shirts or long pants if the Master is in the short version, since the long ones symbolize authority.[65] In fact, the slave should only wear them with the Master's consent. Also, a slave should not wear a collared shirt unless his Master is wearing one. This is why T-shirts, tank tops, or other sleeveless shirts are always safe for a slave.

Footwear is another item to pay attention to. The slave does not wear shoes if his Master is in sandals, nor wear boots if his Master is only in shoes. In general, laced boots are worn with short pants, unlaced with long pants, but one's Master is the final authority on these matters.

Since even when not accompanied by his Master, a slave is meant to be seen only minimally, the slave should not wear anything that would make him stand out. Naturally, there is a certain contradiction to this, in that someone wearing a slave collar is going to stand out from those not collared. But leaving that contradiction aside, a slave should be especially aware of the colors of the clothing appropriate and inappropriate for him. Such noticeable colors are red, pink, orange, bright yellow, bright

---

[65] I personally never like seeing a Master I am with in shorts. Swim trunks are obviously different; although even here a slave may be expected to wear shorter trunks than his Master.

green, turquoise, purple, and red-violet should not be worn by a slave, but confined to the clothes of a Master.

The colors appropriate for a slave are gray,[66] brown, medium to dark blue, olive or khaki green, tan, dark maroon, black,[67] only very subdued yellow, and white, but only in a shirt. Also permissible is a black tie on a white shirt, never a white tie on a black shirt (too attention-getting). Extensive white is not proper unless part of a uniform.

Military or other uniform dress always allows for exceptions. The reason for this is that a uniform is not meant for the wearer to stand out from the crowd but to be seen as uniformly like all the others dressed that way. In other words, dress-wise, the individual is submerged into the collective. However, if a Master and slave are attending some form of fetish wear function, the slave should not be more outstanding than the Master.

It is best for slaves to avoid multi-colors unless they are very dull, which is to say nothing in seriously contrasting shades. Attention-getting patterns or writing on clothing is also un-slave-like, so plain solid colors, hence no stripes or checks, are always the safest.[68]

The slave should not wear flashy ties unless the slave is in a working position that calls for him to wear something like a red "power" tie. If this is the case, then the slave who has a Master should later take the tie to his Master, state the circumstances under which he has needed to wear that color, and receive his permission to do so. Of course, a slave may wear one of the forbidden colors if his Master has, for other reasons, permitted the slave to do so.

The above color issues are largely those for a male slave and would be different for a female slave. In a sexist world, it is more or less expected that a woman will dress with more flash and more erotically than a man, and this also applies to a female slave. The average male Master with a female slave may even want his slave to dress erotically, if not even slightly sluttishly and not like some conservative housewife. Red is the

---

[66] Since gray is a standard business-suit color for all men, his Master will obviously wear such.

[67] Black is a neutral that can be worn by either a Master or a slave.

[68] Some slaves who do not live with the Master may follow these rules even for their bed linen.

color associated with the menstrual cycle, and a female slave in red suggests she is open to her Master or Mistress's sexual wants at any time or place.

The above rule also applies to jackets, leather or otherwise. If the Master has his on, the slave may also. If the Master removes his jacket, not only does the slave, but the slave then holds both jackets.

Some Masters require their slaves to carry some of these slave clothing requirements over into the business world, while some slaves actually volunteer to do this. For those who volunteer, their slave status is a core part of their sense of self, and so every reminder that they are slaves brings a sense of fulfillment and peace. However, this should not go to an extreme. I knew one slave who, taking the issue of trying not to stand out, went too far. He only wore dull gray suits to work. After a month or so, he became the brunt of jokes. In other words, he really stood out. My advice to him was to buy enough different-colored suits that he did not have to wear the same one in a week. He added a black, dark blue, brown, and olive green to his wardrobe, and the jokes stopped.

Also, a slave should wear a tie only if the Master does, and then only with the latter's permission. In other words, no slave should be better or more formally dressed than his Master. This also applies to jewelry, other than piercings. However, for a slave to be more pierced than his Master does draws attention to the slave. On the other hand, some Masters have a fetish for a well-pierced slave.

The preferred jewelry of a slave is his collar and a slave-engraved bracelet[69] or belt buckle; also a stud in his right earlobe (signaling bottom, sub, or slave). This stud may be replaced with a steel or silver letter S stud. Only an alpha slave should wear a gold letter S stud, because gold is worn by Masters, not slaves. However, a lapel pin that color can indicate a training alpha slave. Also, a gaudy watch, especially worn by a slave, is a no-no.

Having said all of the above, there is always the slave who has a fetish for dressing well or fashionably. Since no Master should be foolish enough to demand that such a slave ignore or suppress that fetish, it becomes the

---

[69] This is not the decorative hand-covering chain bracelet that some female submissives or nonsubmissives wear, but a simple steel or silver bar or bar and chain that goes around the wrist and on which the word SLAVE is engraved.

responsibility of both Master and slave to have the Master dress in at least equally high fashion. In other words, the slave may become the master of the Master's wardrobe.

The wearing of caps or hats also involves a protocol ritual. The slave wears a hat or cap only if his Master does or so permits. The Mir (motorcycle or trooper) cap with its visor is generally worn by a Master, while a baseball cap of leather is for an alpha and cloth one is for a non-alpha slave.

Naturally, some Masters have particular clothing fetishes and may want their slave to dress accordingly. For example, one Master I had insisted that when we went to the bar, we were both dressed in the same head-to-toe leather, with the only difference being that I had a heavy collar on and my flogger was on the right (submissive), while his was on the left (dominant).

There may be times when the Master and slave must attend a vanilla formal affair that requires tuxedos. If the attendees would not be surprised by some show of outerwear differentiation, then the Master could wear a red tie or cummerbund, while the beta slave wears a black or gray tie or cummerbund, or an alpha wears a black tie or cummerbund and the gamma a gray one. If such differentiation is deemed as too attention-getting, then both Master and slave would wear the standard black but with some very subtle indication of the slave's status, such as an S lapel pin on the right side. When I have worn that on my lapel and someone not in the know asks me what it means, I decide either to mildly shock them by telling them the truth or, being kinder, I simply say that it is a sigma (the name for the Greek letter s) and refers to a group I belong to, which is also the truth. Those persons mostly assume that means some sort (Greek) fraternity and rarely ask more about it. If they do ask, it is shock time.

It is the slave's responsibility to always be aware of what his Master is going to wear when they are together. If they are to meet somewhere, and the slave does not inquire beforehand as to what the Master would be wearing or ask the Master what the slave should be wearing, the slave has committed a punishable offense.

Also, a slave should never wear cologne or deodorant without his Master's permission. If the Master at any time should decide to use his tongue on his slave, he expects to taste sweat, not some offensive chemical. I made this mistake only once, and to teach me not to do so again, the

Master covered his armpits with one of my most disliked foods and made me lick those armpits clean.

While there are many Masters who have no clue as to how they or slaves should dress, other Masters sadly do not seem to care. But a slave who really prides himself on being the best he can be is naturally going to want a Master who matches him. In this case, if he finds a Master he wants and who wants him, then that slave may have to subtly educate the Master as to how he should masterly dress. Obviously, this must be done with great finesse and never done by lecturing but always by example. For example, the slave who, from the beginning, asks the Master what he is planning on wearing will explain that it would be inappropriate for him (the slave) to wear X either at any time or if the Master is wearing something incompatible. Soon, the sincere Master should start inquiring from the slave what he (the Master) should wear.

Finally, the colors and designs that a slave should not wear should cross over to other items in his life, such as his car. A red, yellow, or gold car should be repainted to a duller color; also, a slave should not be driving a more expensive car than his Master. If he has such a car, he should consider selling it and buying something with a humbler status. A house is an entirely different matter. If a slave has better living conditions than a Master, this will likely affect his relationship sooner or later, and so some creative compromise may be required.

Chapter 16

Undressing and Dressing

Masters can be classified in a number of ways, one of which is how they deal with the unclothing of the slave. The "watcher" is a power-trip ritual that is based on the unspoken threat that, if the slave does not do as commanded, he will be punished. Here the power over the slave is expressed most immediately by the absolutely unbroken stare (voyeuristic power) of the Master. Break the stare, and the power is weakened. At the same time, there is an inherent disadvantage in this watcher ritual, in that the sub, in having the right to undress himself, can be perceived as having a minimum right of independence or freedom from the Master's authority.

The alternative ritual is the "handler." In this, the Master himself carefully strips the fully passively acting slave, which means that slave is allowed absolutely no privacy, since the hand of the Master is always on some part of the slave's body. Here, no necessary threat need be implied; instead, this ritual offers an intimacy lacking in the watcher ritual. The disadvantage to this is that while the eyes of the slave will be continuously on the Master, the Master, unless very careful, could momentarily lose eye contact with the slave as he removes the slave's shoes and pants.

To impress on the Master the slave's submissiveness, before the Master has a chance to make his preference known, the slave can always ask, "Sir, would you prefer me to undress myself or have you do so?" If the slave has his own preference, he can suggest that with a question such as "Sir, do I have your permission to undress myself?" Also, a statement such as, "Sir, as a slave, I do not have the right to undress myself" may work. An even stronger and more direct request could be "Sir. Would it be permissible to ask if Sir would be the one to undress this boy?"

While the nudity of the slave is usually a foregone conclusion, the nudity of the Master is a different issue. In most cases, the Master will remain dressed to some degree until the last minute. One Master I had would always have socks and boots on until he finished with me and was ready to retire. Another Master always made sure he had at least a Master's harness on, especially if the slave had a slave harness on. That same Master knew that I liked to be fucked while wearing boots, and so he also wore them. The main point to this is that while the Master may still have his personal body armor on, the unequaled nudity of the slave is a reminder to that slave that he is entirely exposed to his superior's eyes and authority.[70]

As it is said, however, "Rules are made to be broken," and there are those Masters who prefer to share the nudity with their slave, in which case, to heighten the erotic nature of the mutual nudity of the above watcher/handler, the Master can undress himself while making the slave watch (again a denial of intimacy); or he can order the slave to undress him (a further creating of intimacy). A still further extension of this erotic ritual may occur when the Master and slave have finished playing and are redressing.

The real issue to all of this is intimacy itself. Some Masters feel any intimacy between Masters and slaves weakens the power relationship between the two; other Masters feel it strengthens the bond between the two. Both undressing rituals, if carefully done, can be intensely erotic. So, never underestimate the power of undressing, or for that matter dressing, if another is involved.

Neither a Master nor a slave should be surprised by the fact that many Masters and slaves have clothing fetishes unrelated to specifically erotic wear. This author's most memorable example of this was with a Dom who insisted I come to his place dressed in a business suit with shirt and tie, which was how he was also dressed upon my arrival. He would have me stand while he checked to see that I was properly dressed, from the double knot in my tie to my well- polished shoes.

The Dom, starting with the shoes and moving up, would carefully

---

[70] See Chapter 24. Empowered Humiliation.

remove everything until I was totally naked. With slight pressure on my shoulder, I went down on my knees and licked his shoes before removing them and his socks. There was another licking of his bare feet before I was expected to remove his pants and underwear. After a short sucking on his dick, he had me turn around, and after putting on a condom, he would slap my ass and then fuck me on all fours. All this was done while he still had his shirt, tie, and jacket on. I was then allowed to redress and leave. The whole session never lasted more than forty-five minutes. At no time was there any kissing, and he never touched my dick. It turned out that he believed, sadly, that touching another man's dick would make him less of a Dom.

There were no more visits to this Dom's place, because I missed the affection, missed having my own dick touched and sucked on, and while I found the dressing, undressing, and redressing erotic, it was too much effort for less than an hour of sexual encounter. Also, his footwear was boring.

A far more satisfying clothing-related scene is the intense ritualization of a mutual Master/slave undressing, followed by the Master placing a full (slave) harness on the slave and then the slave placing the half (Dom) harness on the Master, after which the Master and slave may be considered the owner and the owned.[71] This ritual can have a mystical element to it, which comes from the idea that the clothes represent the vanilla world or non-M/s world, while the mutual nude and harnessed state represents a being reborn into the Master/slave world. Rarely is this degree of ritualization done with a one-night Master/slave relationship. It is considered a serious affair, akin to a wedding, and usually goes along with some form of contract signing.

In contrast to either of these is the more or less non-erotic act of a slave undressing while the Master is not paying much attention to the slave by either being busy or undressing himself. One thing a Dom or Master should not do is to leave the room to get toys without leaving behind some symbol of his authority; to do so is to temporarily abandon the slave, which is poor Dom/Master strategy.

Obviously, the opposite of undressing is dressing, and this too can be

---

[71] Unless previously done, this will also be the time that the slave is collared.

part of any relationship, be it Daddy/boy or slave/Master. In the first, the Daddy may choose what the boy is going to wear and then dress him like a parent does a child; but in the second, it is often the slave's responsibility to act valet-like in taking care of the Master's clothes and assisting him in dressing.[72]

In the opinion of this author, the skilled Master will not allow his slave to dress or undress in his presence without his supervision. Likewise, the Master may require the slave to always be present to help him dress and undress. This is certain to reinforce his dominance over his slave.

Before leaving the issue of the power of undressing and redressing, I am reminded of when just such power actually saved me from a gay-bashing. It was late one evening (one to two in the morning), and I had stopped at an off-freeway diner for a quick snack. There were two straight couples there and one lone overweight trucker type, who I assumed drove the truck parked on the side of the diner. He wasn't particularly hot, but be had a beard, a weakness of mine. I looked over at him a couple of times, and he stared back, but not in a gay fashion, so I thought to finish and get out of there in a hurry, although he left before I did.

My car was unfortunately parked next to his truck, and as I was about to get into my car, I felt a hand on my shoulder. Before I could do anything to protect myself, the trucker had me pinned against the side of his truck with his hand tight around my throat. The communication between us went something like this:

"All you faggots like to pick up on straight men, don't you?"

To try to deny I was a faggot would have probably only made him angrier, so I said, "Please, sir! I didn't mean to offend you. I'm sorry."

"Well, faggot, I think I need to teach you a lesson."

We were isolated enough from the other two vehicles, and we were in enough shadows that, even if I could have cried out, nobody would see the crap get beaten out of me, so in desperation, I said, "Sir! Instead of beating me up, you could force me down to service you."

"Just as I thought. That's what you wanted all along."

"I'm good at it. Real good at it, sir."

The fist that he had raised to punch me with came to a halt, and after

---

[72] See Chapter 16. Undressing and Dressing.

looking around to make sure there was no one in view, he said, "One, just one attempt to scream, and it will be your last one. Do you understand?"

"Yes, sir! No screaming."

He slowly let go of his grasp and pushed me down.

I know this was no time to get turned on, but I guess the very danger of my situation made me foolishly hard, which meant manipulating this threat into a scene. As I unbuckled his belt, unbuttoned and unzipped his pants, I said, "Sir! If I'm being forced to do this, it helps to first beat my bare ass with your belt."

"Is that so?"

"Yes, sir!" I didn't even wait for any further words on the subject, as I was already pulling off his belt, to which he didn't protest. I handed him the belt and slowly rose up while undoing my belt, unbuttoning and unzipping my pants, pushing them down. I turned around with my hands pressed against the truck, trying to do all of this as fast as possible so as to not give him time to think, and hence presenting him a done deal. It worked.

He pushed one hand against by my upper back and started whacking me with enthusiasm. When I could take it no more, I called out, "Please, sir! No more. I'll do whatever you want."

A few more whacks, and he stopped. I turned and squatted, carefully pulled down his jeans and then his briefs, took his hard-on into my mouth, and began sucking. As he got close to coming, I had a choice. I could un-mouth it and finish with a hand job, in which case he was going to splatter over my neck and shirt, or I could let him explode in my mouth and then either swallow or spit out. I decided on the last.

It was a good thing for him that we were as isolated as we were, because he wasn't particularly quiet in coming. Before he could recover, I carefully held his dick up by the balls, pulled up his briefs, pulled up his pants, made sure his shirt tails were down before pulling the waist of those pants around him, re-buttoned and re-zipped them, held up my hand, and asked for the belt, which I carefully snaked through the loops and re-buckled. I assumed that this careful attention to redressing him created enough of a bond between us that he wasn't going to hurt me in any way. Nonetheless, to make sure I acknowledged his power over me, and as I pulled myself up, I said, "Please, sir! I've tried my best to make up for any offense to you, so please don't hurt me." While saying this, I made the type of cowardly, defensive face that implied that he might still do so.

Again grabbing my throat, he said, "I'm not going to hurt you, man, but don't you ever give another guy like me the look you did in the diner, because the next guy might not be as forgiving. Now get your fairy ass into your car, and get the hell out of here before I change my mind."

I wanted to say *I still think you're a hot man,* but I didn't want to press my luck and instead said, "Yes, sir! Thank you, sir!" And with that, I did as I was told.

Chapter 17

Slave Collars

There is no absolutely agreed-upon category of slave collars. Some Masters view a collar as a collar, with the only difference being that one is simply a locked chain or locked leather band around a slave's neck. Other Masters have gradient collars such as probationary, level-one training, level-two training, and permanent. Each of these may be color coded. My probationary collar was an inexpensive collar for a large dog that had a buckle but no lock. This was only placed on me during the times when I was with the Master; the rest of the time, I was left with just the chain around my neck that had a lock. This was only removed in emergency situations, for example, going through airport security; if I needed it removed, I had to notify the Master in advance.

I should mention that on occasion, rather than an ordinary locked chain or leather training collar, I was required to wear a large steel dog-training collar with blunted spikes on the inside (pinch collar). Each time the Master pulled on the front chain, the spikes would press into the back and sides of my neck. The spikes being blunted avoided dermal penetration and any flow of blood. The whole point of the collar was simply for an "ouch!"

As a fully trained slave, there were times I wore a locked leather collar along with the locked chain. Once I became an alpha, I was allowed to wear a locked black leather collar with red piping.[73] However, some Masters allow any fully trained slave to wear this.

The wearer of an unlocked collar needs clarification, as it can simply mean that the person is not probationary, much less owned, but in search of a Master. To signal that the collar wearer has no Master but is looking for one, the lock can be replaced by a double spring clip.

An alternative to wearing a collar is for the slave who is wearing a jacket with epaulets to have a chain or leather collar under the right arm, threaded through the epaulet, indicating he is looking for a Master. A collar on the opposite side would be for a Master looking for a slave.

With all present-day security devices for detecting metal, including chain collars, the slave needs to be creative, and one way is if the slave expects to go through a series of such devices and does not want his collar removed one or more times, he and/or his Master might consider a small linked plastic chain for temporary use.

A collar may be of special importance at those times when a slave reconnects with his Master after being away from him for any significant time. For example, after the slave comes home from work, a "home collar" might go on him as soon as he can kneel before the Master. This collar, which is never worn by the slave if he is not with the Master, can serve to remind the slave that whatever authority over him he experienced at work (from a boss or bosses) is now in the past, and only the Master's authority is real. Also, it is customary that when changing from one collar to another, the new one goes on before the old one comes off; this way the slave is not, even momentarily, un-collared (un-slaved).

Whatever kind of collar a slave wears, it should be loose enough (1) for easy breathing, especially if he is going to sleep in it; (2) for his Master to be able to grab hold of it to pull his slave toward him; and (3) not to interfere in the slave's ability to fellate the Master.

One important aspect about wearing a collar is that it should never be put on or taken off a slave without some ritual or ceremony involved. To be too casual in this is to denigrate the submission process.

Some slaves, due to work or family situations, cannot wear a collar full time, even one that can pass for jewelry. This is even true for some female

---

[73] See Chapter 15. Slave Wear II (colors).

slaves, since no woman wears the same necklace 24/7, month after month, without drawing attention to herself. In this case, a wrist chain or ankle chain might need to be substituted for the times she is not in private with her Master.

Chapter 18

Blindfolds and Hoods

While the first of these would only be worn by a submissive, the second can be worn by either a submissive or a Dominant. The hood of the sub, however, will often have a removable blindfold with it. Blindfolding a sub is an intense act of domination for two reasons. First, it leaves the sub unable to know what to expect from the Dom. Second, when a sub's eyes cannot meet the Dom's eyes, there is a far greater sense of depersonalization of the sub. In other words, the sub becomes more of an "it" than a "he." Never put a blindfold on someone wearing contact lenses; it may press those into the eyes.

The hood on the Dom likewise serves to depersonalize him, as far as the sub is concerned, which further depersonalizes the sub, even if he is not hooded, because a person's face more than any other part of the body gives that person his identity, his uniqueness. When that identity is hidden behind a hood, the power exchange between the Dom and sub can radically change. In fact, many Masters feel that having themselves hooded gives them a greater sense of power over their sub, and this is even more intensified if the sub is also hooded and blindfolded.

Remember also that blindfolds and hoods act as sensory-deprivation items, which for both the Master and slave can intensify the erotic experience.

Chapter 19

Wearing Gloves

In some traditions, only Masters are expected to wear gloves, but in colder climates, this is simply impractical. So, if a slave may wear gloves, he should do so only if his Master is wearing them, and should the Master remove one or more glove, so must the slave. Also, if a slave is wearing gloves, they should not be of leather, but wool, which should be removed in the rare event that he is allowed to shake the hand of a Master other than his own. The reason for this is simple: a gloved hand is a symbol of authority, and for a slave to offer his own gloved hand to a Master is pretentious. If the slave is not wearing gloves and it is cold, he may, with the Master's permission, put his hands in his jacket pockets or his back, never front, pants pockets, since this forces the slave's shoulders forward in a defeatist stance. I was dating one Master during January and February, and although he normally didn't wear gloves even then, he knew that I had a hatred of the cold, and so when we were out, he purposely wore gloves so I could. Remember, a slave should not be more clothed than his Master.

One other possibility is that a slave may wear mittens, which do not carry the authority that gloves do. The problem with mittens is that they are often worn by the bottom in animal scenes, to give the bottom paws. So, if the bottom doesn't want to be perceived as a possible animal of his Master/Owner, mittens might not be a good idea. On the other hand, mittens are sometimes put on a bottom as a form of sensory deprivation. It is hard to feel one's own body or that of the Top with them on.

In some traditions, the slave does not hold the gloves or hat/cap of the Master, but in the one that I am most familiar with, the slave holds anything the Master takes off.

The above description has nothing necessarily to do with "glove fetishism," in which the gloves themselves cause erotic arousal.

Chapter 20

Harnesses

There are two categories of harnesses, the Top or half harness, and the bottom or full harness. The simplest half harness is one in which a leather or chain strap goes around the chest (just below the pecs) and back and is held up by a right and left shoulder strap that may or may not cross each other. More complex half harnesses add more straps. This Top harness may be used for the bottom/sub/slave to hold on to if he and his Master are moving through a crowded room or even when the slave is on his back and is getting fucked. Unfortunately, a lot of pseudo-Tops wear this to be fashionable.

The full harness can also be of leather and/or chains. It is like the half harness, only there is a front and back vertical strap, usually leading to one or more pairs of lower horizontal straps and a second vertical strap leading to a cock ring. There may be a further strap that goes from the cock ring through the legs and between the buttocks to connect to the lowest horizontal strap that surrounds the waist. While this is a basic description, some bottom harnesses can be even more elaborate, especially if connected to a collar. The only universal rule seems to be that in a bottom, sub, or slave harness, the cock ring is attached to whatever is above it. This full harness is useful for the Top to grab hold of the bottom in a display of ownership or at least temporary dominance. The all-chain sub harness, while not the most comfortable, mimics chain bondage, which for some subs is extremely erotic.

While most harnesses are of leather and/or chain, there are rope harnesses, but these cannot be put on and taken off at a moment's notice unless they are cut. The huge length of rope used for them is expensive, and the time it takes to weave them onto the wearer makes their wearing rare. However, I knew a Master rope artist who put me into several of his creations. One was an elaborate slave harness in black rope, which allowed for the rope line going up the back by way of the buttocks to be instantly released, so the wearer could either shit or get fucked without having to remove any other part of the harness. It was hot! Another harness had the entire chest covered in an elaborate Celtic knot/dreamcatcher pattern that was the awe of everyone who saw it.

One other category of harness is the bondage harness, in which the upper and sometimes lower arms are secured by straps to the torso harness, restricting the movement of the arms. I was put in one of these only once by a trusted Dom who knew I could be a fighter and wanted to tame me before he forced me to suck him off.

Caution: never let anyone put you into a bondage harness, or any bondage, that does not have one or more "panic snaps," a way of instantly releasing the person from bondage in case of an emergency.

Chapter 21

Hair

Hair, whether head or facial, is a sign of authority in many cultures. In particular, facial hair has been associated with male adulthood and even a status of freedom. In either a Daddy/boy or a Master/slave pairing, it is very rare for a boy or slave to have a beard if the Daddy or Master is clean-shaven. In the traditional Master/slave case, the Master often requires the slave to not only to be clean-shaven but to keep his head hair shorter than that of the Master, and it is not unheard of for the Master to keep the slave's head shaved. Of course, there are those Masters who have hair fetishes and want the slave, if not himself, to sport long hair or a beard. One Master I knew had a thing for scalp locks and mohawks.

A former Master was clean-shaven and did not even like beards, but in the negotiations, I accepted that if I refused to shave it off, I would be subject to daily punishment for that refusal (rebelliousness). It was placed in the contract that at least once a day (sometimes twice if we had sex that day), I would have my bearded face slapped on each side one to three times. On other occasions, while having dinner, the Master would push my face (beard) into my plate of food and tell me that that was a small price for the right to keep the beard.

Both my current Master and I have beards and think that any man looks better (more erotic) with one.

Chapter 22

Tattooing and Other Bodily Modifications

I will not go into all the possible bodily modifications M/s people can get into, since (a) there are too many of them, and (b) I have experiences with only three of these (tattoos, brands, and piercings). While both Masters and slaves often have tattoos and piercings, only a rare number of subs and slaves will have been branded. In any of these cases, safety and expertise should be the absolute requirement. It is not uncommon to see a tattooed and/or pierced sub/slave and a non-tattooed or pierced Dom or Master, while it is far less common to see the reverse. Just as there are many reasons to be tattooed or pierced, there are many reasons *not* to be. No slave should ever be required or pressured into being tattooed, pierced, or in other ways subjected to any form of body modification. To do so is *abuse*.

If both a Master and a slave are tattooed, it is not uncommon for each to have some tattoo, even a very tiny one that signifies their respective status. It could be as simple as a larger capital M on the Master and a smaller s on the sub/slave.

Piercings are a different matter. As mentioned earlier, the most common bottom, sub, or slave piercing is of his right earlobe. This complements that of a Top, Dom, or Master who may have his left earlobe pierced. Most other piercings are status neutral.

Branding is totally different from tattooing and requires an expertise beyond that of an ordinary tattooist. The uninformed too often think that a branding on human skin will look like that on a horse or steer. It will not. Those animals have much thicker skin (hides) than a human being does, and all that the brand does it to permanently remove any hair on that hide. Unlike any tattoo, a brand on human flesh forms a scar that spreads as it heals, and if sufficient space is not left between the lines in a design, the whole thing will merge into an unrecognizable scarred mess. For this reason, most letters should be avoided, because there is not enough room between their lines unless the brand is huge.[74] Also, whereas getting a tattoo has become far more socially acceptable, the same cannot be said of getting a brand. Before a sub or slave decides to get one, he should make sure he is not going to be socially ostracized for it in the present or future. To reduce that possibility, he might be better off if any brand is where only a Dom or Master would see it, but not likely anyone else. Also, like a tattoo, it is better to avoid being too specific in its meaning, so that in the future, one can reinterpret its significance. Also remember, having a tattoo removed is expensive, but having a brand (scar) removed is very expensive, as in surgery.

---

[74] Thus, a two-liner like T (Toy, Thrall, Tamed, cock Taker, Trash, Trick, peT, SluT, or L Leather, love, lust, sLave) or V (V-slaVe, Vassel), or O (Owned, Obeys) would be best.

Chapter 23

Punishment (Non-erotic Discipline)

No v-slave gets punished who does not agree to be punished. This having been said, genuine slave punishment can be defined as something that is usually unpleasant to the slave but not always painful and which a slave must accept for doing what he is not supposed to do or not doing what he is supposed to do. The term *genuine* is used here to distinguish it from that less-than-genuine punishment that a few slaves may be subject to because of something they did so that they could be punished. This is punishment play and just a variety of SM. If the Master is aware that this is going on, that is okay, but if he is not, then the slave is dishonestly manipulating the Master and is a questionable slave.[75]

Before going into the punishment itself, it should be understood that most Masters are not interested in doing a lot of punishing because it takes time and energy away from them being served by the slave. A slave who requires more than an occasional punishment is probably going to be dropped by the Master. The exception is the Master who is into being abusive and/or may have a slave who is into being abused.

With regards to punishment itself, Masters can be divided into two categories. There is the majority type, who only punish for a refusal to obey an order. In this case, the slave who makes a mistake is expected to admit it, to honestly say he is sorry, to promise to try never to make it again, and to ask for a pardon, usually on his knees. One thing the slave should

---

[75] See Chapter 44. Manipulating the Master.

never do is immediately make an excuse, justifiable or not, for his mistake. Rather than automatically coming to his own defense, he should either wait until the Master asks for an excuse or at the most ask the Master if he wants to hear the excuse.[76]

The second type of Master, the minority type, believes that the best way to train a slave is to give him very little preliminary direction, allowing him to make a lot of mistakes, and then punish him for each of them. But this Master also knows that each slave is a unique person and must be trained as such. Therefore, the heavy hand he may use on one slave should not be used on another. Some might regard this second type of Master as abusive, but I would argue that a more masochistic slave can greatly benefit from this Master, as long as he does not evolve into the Master from hell.

The Master from hell is the one who tends to treat all slaves the same way and expects from his slave or slaves more than the slave(s) may be able to give. He thus drives the slave to exhaustion and eventual escape, since no slave should tolerate this way for long. This Master, more often than not, out of either insecurity or sadism or both, is afraid to be seen as too weak in his disciplinary function and compensates by abusive disciplining. Also, this Master does not know the difference between being a Dominant and domineering. The Dominant knows the difference between subtle control and brute force; between well-thought-out erotic discipline and punishment (non-erotic discipline); between trying to understand his slave's deeper needs versus only his more superficial ones; between wanting the slave to grow into his slavery versus wanting an unchanging slave who is no threat to being the Master's property. The confident Master is aware that he is fallible while the Master from hell at least wants to believe he is infallible and will only attract an insatiable masochistic slave or be cursed with a really bad slave from hell.[77]

While too much punishment suggests a too-sadistic Master and/or one who is very insecure about the loyalty of his slave, too little punishment can also mean insecurity, but of a Master who does not think himself sure enough to know when to and when not to punish; or even worse, it can

---

[76] This is another way of distinguishing a mere submissive from a slave. The first has every right to automatically come to his own defense.

[77] See Chapter 43. Maintaining the M/s Relationship.

imply the Master's loss of interest in his slave. In other words, the balance between too much and too little punishment is the desired goal; such a balance or lack of it can be one aspect of how healthy an M/s relationship is.

Before any kind of punishment is administered, a Master should find out if the offense was due to true negligence or a way for the slave to get attention from the Master. Yes, sometimes a slave seeks out punishment for the latter reason. Determining which of these is the case should also determine the nature and severity of the punishment. Whenever punishment is used, the Master should always ask himself, "Will this enhance the bond between me and my slave, or will it do the opposite?"

Punishment need not involve any kind of pain. In fact, there are going to be prospective slaves who, for any number of reasons, cannot accept pain, such as those who have no masochistic tendencies or have experienced an abusive past that they do not want resolved through further pain.[78] Still, such individuals want to be and might make good slaves domestically and/ or sexually. For such slaves, there are a variety of punishments that while physically pain-free are no less effective as punishment, for example:

(1) The Master demands nothing more than that the slave kneel humbly in front of his Master in acknowledgment that he (the slave) has done something wrong (violated protocol) and wishes to apologize and seek a pardon for it.

(2) The Master requires the slave to do five to twenty pushups, depending on his physical ability.

(3) The slave, from a kneeling position, is required to get down on his belly to kiss the feet of the Master, then back up and back down ten to twenty times; of course, for a slave who has never exercised, this and the previous punishment could technically be called physically painful.

(4) The slave is made to stand facing a corner and/or having to write down on a pad of paper "I will not disobey my Master" one hundred, two hundred, or more times, like a naughty child.

(5) The slave will have tape put over his mouth for a few hours, be made to wash his own mouth out with his own piss, or wear a

---

[78] However, many slaves who have experienced an involuntary-abuse past actually seek to resolve that past with voluntary pain.

gag for several hours, especially one saturated in his own or the Master's piss. These two are punishment for either shouting at the Master or saying no to him when it should have been yes.

(6) The slave is required to move around on all fours for part of the day.

(7) The slave is made to eat either sitting on the floor or standing up rather than having the privilege of sitting down with the Master.

(8) The slave is required to wear handcuffs and/or ankle restraints for a day.

(9) The slave is made to do toilet-paper service for the Master for a whole day. In this, the slave has to wipe his Master's ass each time the Master takes a shit. This is usually done with a glove on, but not always. This is not to be confused with a Daddy/boy situation in which the Daddy is into treating his boy as an infant (a diaper Daddy).

(10) The slave is required to wash out the toilet or tub or scrub the whole bathroom floor on his knees. This is a punishment assigned to a sexual-only slave, since a domestic slave might do this as a regular part of his housekeeping services.

(11) The slave is made to read a book out loud that the Master likes, but the slave has no interest in, or worse, hates.

(12) The slave is denied his favorite food for a week.

For a creative Master, there is no end to the possibilities for nonphysical pain-involved punishments, and one of these should always be preferred over something physically painful, because a Master who is mostly into physical punishment is certainly more interested in abusive dominance than in developing a power-exchange relationship with his slave.[79]

Some of the above forms of non-pain punishment may not seem like punishment to a non-slave but will to genuine slave. No honest slave wants to disappoint his Master, and that he has to do something he does not like because of it is in itself punishment.

One absolute rule is that a punishable offense should not go unpunished,

---

[79] This is a "thinly disguised child abuse done by an overaged child." Guy Baldwin, *Ties that Bind.*

nor should they be delayed for more than is absolutely necessary. As mentioned above, an unpunished violation may suggest a Master who is weak, who is too lazy to fulfill his responsibilities, or who is growing indifferent to the relationship.

Painless punishment can be especially useful to prevent the use of painful punishment from backfiring on a Master, especially if he has mistakenly contracted with an extremely masochistic slave who may disobey or otherwise act out often in order to receive a painful punishment. In this case, painless punishment may result in the masochistic slave seeking a more brutal Master.

A special kind of punishment, one that should be rarely used, consists of some version of "purely authority sex punishment"—where the slave either is required to milk himself or is milked by the Master, to de-eroticize the slave, after which there would be sexual demands made on the sexually uninterested slave, which could include a non-erotic flogging. In other words, it was sex mainly to reestablish the Master's authority over the slave.

Such post ejaculation punishment should not include anal penetration (the Master fucking the slave) without the Master offering at least two other reasonable alternatives. Otherwise, such penetration might be considered the equivalent of rape. Such punishment sex can occur as a result of the slave having no justifiable reason for previously saying no to the Master's sexual advances.[80]

Whatever kind of punishment is used, the Master must always follow this with "aftercare."[81] In this case, it means that the Master leaves no doubt in the slave's mind that the punishment has cleared the slate; that all is forgiven, and that there should be no feelings of lingering guilt or shame on the part of the slave. A Master who fails to do this successfully is going to end up with a less-than-optimal slave.

The most argued-about punishment in the M/s Scene is whether or not a slave should be punished for the mistakes or wrongs of his Master. There is rarely a Master who, at some point, does not do something wrong that

---

[80] My one such experience with this de-eroticized fuck was when I said no to a Master simply because I was angry with him. Not a justifiable reason for denying him his right to be.

[81] See more on this below under Chapter 34. Aftercare.

should require at least apologizing to the slave. If it is a minor wrong, the Master might simply say "Sorry," and that's the end of it. However, with a more serious mistake, the Master may not be able to get off so easily. An apology may certainly be in order, but that apology may put the Master in a compromised position as far as his authority goes—that is to say, a temporarily surrendering of some of his dominance if that same mistake made by the slave required punishment. One way to deal with this is that the slave is ordered to his knees as the Master apologizes, and the slave accepts such an apology with a humble "This slave thanks his Master for allowing this slave to accept his Master's apology." [82]

The Master, by definition, cannot be punished for his mistakes, and certainly not by the slave, other than through some passive-aggressive action on the part of the slave. Therefore, the Master would have to find a senior Master to punish him, or the slave must take the punishment (be the whipping boy) for his Master. This punishment, however, must be genuine, which means it cannot be of a kind that is erotically desired by either the Master or the slave. It must, therefore, be a punishment that the Master genuinely feels bad (guilty) about imposing on the innocent slave. Obviously, this sounds like nothing short of abuse of the Master's power over the slave, but it need not be so.

The wise and just Master is required by M/s justice protocol to punish a punishable offense even for the Master's own mistakes. However, the Master knows that to punish his slave for those mistakes automatically puts the Master into debt to the slave. The just Master always pays his debts, at least if he wants to keep his slave. The slave, perfectly aware of this justice payment system, has every right, while being punished, to think about what reward (payment) he is going to expect from the Master. [83] Perhaps the Master already knows what the slave will want, and if not, he will skillfully inquire in such a way as to not admit the real reason for his generosity. This payment/reward/compensation is never openly acknowledged as such by either the Master or slave; it is, instead, treated as an unearned gift of the Master to the slave, for which the slave shows surprised appreciation.

---

[82] For light apologies, such as if a Master accidentally bumps into the slave and says "Sorry," the slave's response might be a "Of nothing, Sir."

[83] See Chapter 44. Manipulating the Master.

To further ensure that the fairness of this system is not abused, the Master, in this case, may well offer the slave a choice of punishments, two or three, in which one may be heavier than the other(s). This may allow the slave to pick the punishment that he feels will maximize his reward, perhaps much to the regret of the Master.

Naturally, this process of the slave getting punished for the Master's mistakes is easily open to corruption and abuse, but it is only likely to happen if the Master is deliberately making mistakes in order to punish the slave. This should soon become obvious to the slave and result in him bolting.

The above verse may seem playfully ridiculous, but it is not. While slaves are perfectly aware that Masters can and do make any number of mistakes, the skillful slave will try to adopt the "convenient fiction or noble lie" mind-set. This is a belief or attitude that, while serving a psychologically or morally constructive purpose (hence being convenient or noble), on close scrutiny, it is shown to be logically incompatible either with the greater and possibly more logical parts of some other belief or logically incompatible with commonly accepted truth as a whole (hence a fiction or a lie). In traditional (legal) slavery, the Master can do any number of things wrong that need no apology, because the slave has no power to protest, much less dump the Master. In voluntary slavery, it is the opposite, therefore, some mechanism for mistakes with real consequences needs to be in place, and the convenient fiction mind-set is one such mechanism.

I knew a slave who got into an argument with his Master over something the slave regarded as totally offensive. He felt the Master should have known that and never done it, but the Master did. The slave was so enraged that no mere apology would do. It was either punishment or break up. The solution that the slave chose was to be flogged, but not erotically. This meant he had to ejaculate (be milked) first, thereby eliminating any eroticism from the punishment, and as a result, the flogging was exclusively one of pain. The Master, feeling so bad about it, quietly cried throughout the punishment. The breach was healed, and the slave was rewarded. Another time, a Master broke verbal protocol by accidentally calling the slave *dear*. Such a language endearment is corrupting to the Master/slave relationship by bringing vanilla language or language of equality into it.[84] Remember that an hour of vanilla talk can ruin a whole day of M/s talk, and a whole day of vanilla talk can corrupt a whole week of M/s talk. Both Master and slave must learn or even be conditioned (often by each other) to avoid such language, and one way this is done is by having the slave's mouth washed out with soap each time it happens, regardless of who the offending party is. But again, the slave must be rewarded if it was the Master's fault.

An important aspect of punishment that should not be overlooked is delayed punishment credit (DPC). There are times when a slave may receive unearned punishment or the punishment has been out of proportion to the violation. In this case, the slave and Master may need to negotiate DPC, which is to say, apply a past surplus of punishment to a present or future situation that will lessen or even eliminate the need for the latest punishment.

An important aspect of this process is that every slave and Master should avoid any unnecessary public talk about the punishment that the slave receives or does not receive. This is a private matter, and unless the slave feels he is being abused, he should direct all outside questions about his punishment to his Master, who will decide to answer it or not.

The obvious exception to this is if the slave has to accept public punishment that may be required if the slave does something inappropriate in front of others in the Scene. For example, if the slave violates protocol by speaking out when he should be silent, by being too familiar with another Master, or by any other action that may suggest that his Master has not properly trained the slave. To save face, private punishment may not do. The slave may need to be publicly put in his place, which should include his public confessing of his wrongdoing.

This brings us to the most important aspect of slavehood. It is not just submitting to the Master's will; nor is it the receiving of punishment that should be foremost in a person's desire to be a slave. In fact, if punishment alone is what a person is seeking, this can be gained in any number of simple non-slave playing ways. Rather it is a potential slave's desire for

---

[84] See Chapter 43. Maintaining the M/s Relationship.

self-discipline and the freedom that can bring him that should be most important.

Caution: For anyone playing with a Dom or Master for the first time, do not ignore "informed consent." This is not just consent, but being told by the Dom or Master the kind of erotic discipline, the intensity of that discipline, and the things that could go wrong with that discipline he is planning on subjecting you to. If you do not require this, then what the Dom may regard as voluntary discipline, the sub may regard as involuntary punishment (non-erotic discipline).

Chapter 24

Empowering (Erotic) Humiliation

The subject of humiliation in the Master/slave relationship is a controversial issue, and before entering into it, one thing must be made absolutely clear: slave humiliation and ridicule are not the same. What is the difference? For the purpose of slave protocol, ridicule is an attack on the very value and being, the self-worth of the slave, and any Master who ridicules a slave is admitting that he (the Master) is incapable of understanding the worth of that slave and every human being, which includes himself. Proper protocol humiliation never serves to alienate a slave from himself or the Master, but to strengthen the bond of authority between Master and slave. To make sure of this, the types and limitations of humiliation should always be negotiated before any scene and clearly stated in any M/s contract. Remember, however, that one person's erotic, empowering, and consenting humiliation may seem to another abusive ridicule. Also, what may be empowering in private can easily become ridicule in public; so should not be advertised.

There is always one situation in which seemingly innocent humiliation can result in debilitation. This is during repeated SM scenes in which the sub or slave enters an altered state of consciousness and is no longer able to distinguish fantasy play from reality. In this state, the sub/slave's subconscious might accept whatever humiliating language as true of him. This is especially the case for a sub/slave who, for whatever reason, has a low self-worth. In this way, what might be empowering humiliation becomes disempowering ridicule.

A simple way of distinguishing ridicule from humiliating play language is to decide whether or not the language would amount to insults to the slave's normal core identity. Calling someone a moron, an idiot, or stupid, telling a slave he is incompetent, even comparing him unfavorably with another slave are all forms of ridicule and serve no other purpose than to alienate the slave from himself and from the Master. When this happens, the slave should ask himself why this Master would want such a piece of crap. Maybe it is because that is all this Master thinks he can get for a slave.

The secret to erotic empowering humiliation is that the Master and sub equally know that it is pure fantasy and it is not to be tolerated otherwise. For this reason, until a slave develops sufficient trust in a Master, it is best for both parties to stay away from any humiliating language related to race, ethnicity, culture, religion, physical appearance or body parts, deformities, sexual orientation, and intelligence levels. Remember, the amount of trust required between a Master and slave needs to be much greater than that between a couple who regard each other as equals. This requires that the sub makes it perfectly clear what he will and will not tolerate as far as humiliation goes. In other words, this is not a power to be given to the Master.

The question, of course, is why does a Master *ever* humiliate a slave, and why does a slave ever accept humiliation? The common assumption by the community outside of the Master/slave one, both straight and gay, is that this giving and receiving is only done by individuals who are "suffering" from a severely low self-image. In my years in the Master/slave community, I have found that there are, indeed, such low-self-image individuals, both as slaves and Masters, but far more slaves and Masters I have known have very high self-images, and I include myself in that group. Proof of all of this can be found by observing especially the slave, in his non-slave situation in the outside world. While most slaves are closeted about their slave status, this does not prevent many of them from being successful businessmen and -women, politicians, judges, lawyers, doctors, teachers, etc. These far from having low self-esteem individuals are society's role models of high self-esteem persons, and wearing a dog collar or even being referred to as the Master's dog in private does not lower the slave's self-esteem, because the slave knows that if the Master really wanted a dog

(*Canis familiaris*), he would go to an animal shelter to get one.[85] This is true even for those scenes in which the sub puts on animal wear and plays the part. The Master and slave are still very aware that the sub is still human. Any slave who feels he is being ridiculed as a dog has a responsibility to advise the Master of this as the slave shuts the door in the Master's face.

Under the chapter "Slave Protocol (Definitions)," there was a good deal about the meaning of the term "boy." There it was pointed out that outside of a very selective group of individuals, one does not call an adult man a boy unless you mean to offend him. Obviously, this is because to do so is to challenge both his adult masculinity and to imply that he is socially lower than the speaker. Even after the end of legal slavery in the United States, black men in the segregated South would still be called "boys" in a clear attempt to challenge their masculinity and any right to social equality. This was "disempowering or a robbing of power" language, if for no other reason than that no black man gave a white person the right to call him *boy*.

When a slave "gives" a Master the right to call him a boy, he is, to one degree or another, voluntarily giving up or offering up some or all of his power to "combine" with that of the Master. The Master's power has now been enhanced, but the slave can take that power back at any time, which actually gives the slave a certain power over the Master that the slave did not have until he gave away or loaned out his submissive power. In this sense, not only has the Master's power been enhanced by the receiving the slave's power, the slave's power has been enhanced by giving it. Should the slave and Master, in time, separate, the slave still retains the power that made a Master, while the Master, in turn, is left with a power that made a slave. In other words, the slave and Master have made a profit on the slave's loan and the Master's acceptance of that loan. This is why the process should be called a mutual "power exchange" and part of that exchange can be "empowering humiliation."[86]

I have actually heard some in the Master/slave community say there is no humiliation involved in their Master/slave relationship, to which I

---

[85] Kennel or puppy (and other animal) play is a special fantasy game separate from the Master/slave one.

[86] See Chapter 45. Love and Romance.

always reply, the moment one person (a Master) says that he owns another person (a slave), there is humiliation involved. In other words, the very designation "slave" universally implies some sort of humiliation, even if that designation is voluntary.

Besides the above power exchange, we might ask, "What are some of the more specific reasons a man or woman of high self-esteem might choose to accept periodic humiliation?" That question I cannot answer for anyone other than myself. For me, it entails:

(1) Communicating to the Dominant that I trust him in a way that less extreme words or actions cannot communicate.

(2) A sense of surrendering my "outside" ego and responsibility for myself, as much as it is practically possible for me.

(3) A disappearing of myself into the Master, in which I am no longer myself but what he tells me I am.

(4) The giving of a gift of extra power to the Master which, paradoxically, is a way of making the Master partially dependent on me. "So much for totally surrendering of my ego." But then, in every top-quality Master, there is a tiny bit of submissiveness; and in every top-quality slave, there should be a tiny bit of dominance.

(5) An intensifying of the pleasure-pain sexual experience that simple vanilla does not offer. On the other hand, erotic humiliation can be especially useful in dominance-submissive situations in which no real physical force or pain, no real SM, is involved. In this case, the psychological dominance of the Master is so thorough, so absolute, that the sex itself may be completely vanilla. A Master who can achieve this level of psychological dominance is rare.

Along with all the other parts of the negotiations between a potential Master and slave, the type and degree of humiliation that a Master might give and a slave accept must be taken very seriously and never be overlooked or minimized. Surprises in this matter can completely negate everything that has been negotiated and may automatically void the contract.

In fact, beware of surprises! Often a Master will go out of his way to come up with some act that he thinks will push a slave into proving just how far the slave will go in obeying that Master. This author's most extreme experience in this regard was when he was still in the dating phase of seeing a Master, so no negotiations, much less contract, had been finalized; however, the third time I was at the Master's home, he insisted that after he shit, this slave should be the one to wipe his ass. Now, I knew of this toilet-paper service requirement, but only as a punishment by humiliation for a slave's serious infraction; but as I was still not formally his slave, nor had I done anything to be punished for, I assumed this was a test to see how far I would go to obey. Also, I wasn't sure whether this was a one-time test or something more, but hoping for the former, this slave said, "Sir! Am I being asked to do this without a glove?"

"Do you have a problem with that?"

"Sir! This is something that only a contracted slave might be required to do, and since my service to you has not yet been contractually formalized, the use of a glove seems appropriate. I am fully aware that you might find my reluctance to serve you without a glove as an offense, but as still uncontracted, I have a problem with this."

If any such service as this is stated in the contract, it should be performed, otherwise it need not be. However, if a slave is not willing to do one humiliating or self-deprecating act for a potential Master, then he may not be cut out to be a slave.

On the other hand, this is not to imply in any way that a slave should do anything that might endanger his health or safety, which is why this author had every right to negotiate for a glove.[87]

The Master, in the above situation, settled for a glove, and the very fact that he had a whole box of them right behind the toilet told me that I was not the first to negotiate on this ass-wiping issue. However, since a fecal fetish was not the trip of this slave, he had no more play dates with this Master.

When dealing with erotic humiliation, a distinction should be made between what happens with a stranger (a one-night stand) and a long-term partner. The first may be easily forgotten the next day, the second not so. Therefore, the Master has to be far more careful about how he plays with humiliation than the stranger does. A Master must always remember that what he may actually think is only a minor humiliation, the slave may regard as major damage to his slave pride. On the other hand, a Master

---

[87] See Chapter 28. Safe Sex vs. Bodily-Fluid Exchange.

who really knows and appreciates his slave can creatively use erotically empowering humiliation to intensify the bond between him and his slave.

The humiliation issue can be used to make another distinction between a Master/slave and a Daddy/boy relationship. I knew of a Daddy/boy pair in which it was the Daddy who insisted on wiping the boy's ass after toileting. This was not in any way designed as an act of humiliation, but a form of age play in which the boy takes on the role of a child and/or is infantilized. The Daddy may also insist on keeping his boy shaved of pubic hair. This is in no way to be confused with pedophilia. The boy here is always an adult, hence teleiophilia,[88] and can be one of any age, including older than the Daddy.

As far as humiliation goes, the language used between a Master and slave can be a very sensitive issue. This humiliating language is more than just the more common sexually arousing "dirty talk" between partners. In most Master/slave encounters, the humiliating language is directed toward and accepted by a slave, but the reverse, although rare, might be the case. For example, one black Master I was told about liked to say to his white slave, "Does this boy like his nigger Master shoving his shooter up his white slave shithole?" The boy was expected to respond with "Yes, Sir! This boy likes his nigger Master shoving his shooter up his white slave shithole."

In a culture where historically whites have always held the dominant rank and blacks the subordinate rank, the Master and his slave were not simply reversing those ranks; instead, by using that derogatory word, they were intensifying that reversal. The Master, by calling himself a nigger, was humiliating himself with the word, and in doing so was doubly humiliating his white property, who was now not just a white being fucked by a black, but a white being fucked by a nigger. The result of this was a kind of doubling of the erotic submission of the slave to the Master.

In another case of "reversals," I knew of a female Jewish slave whose Master always wore a Nazi uniform during their sex; this, as in the above case, demonstrates first that neither a cock nor a cunt understands political correctness, and second, that erotic humiliation is not exclusively gay but can be part of both the straight and lesbian SM Scene.

As a final note on this issue of humiliation, it should be emphasized

---

[88] Love of adults, hence the opposite of pedophilia.

that a proud slave does not grovel. Groveling is submitting to humiliation (often an act of kneeling or being on all fours) to gain the approval of someone you really don't like and would rather have nothing to do with, but repugnant circumstances have forced you into this position to gain or avoid something. If a slave feels he is groveling before his Master, he should immediately think of getting out of that relationship.

Caution: For anyone playing with a Dom or Master for the first time, be honest with him about humiliation. If it turns you off, just tell him you are not used to that kind play language and feel uncomfortable with it. This should be enough for him to get the message.

To summarize, a sincere Master/slave bond humiliation must never be mistaken for or evolve into either ridicule or groveling.

Chapter 25

Slave Pride and Master Pride

An important thing to know about being a slave is that "a good slave" is a proud slave. In a less-than-tolerant society toward kink, there are a number of reasons for keeping one's slave feelings, much less any Master/slave relationship, from all but the most understanding and trustworthy, but one reason a true slave should never hide is because he is ashamed of wanting to be a slave. Any such shame (a) will lead to being a very poor slave, and/ or (b) will open one up to attracting an abusive Master who is more than willing to abuse the slave who is ashamed. A slave with genuine pride in himself will never allow any Master to abuse him. In fact, the proud slave knows that such a Master is himself filled with shame and only seeks out a slave to help relieve himself of some of that shame by trying to transfer it onto the slave.

In a society that equates submissiveness with contempt, especially if it is a man who is voluntarily offering to be submissive, it is obvious why that man might feel ashamed. When the word *slave* is added to this, the shame element is at least doubled. This means that the man who does not have a strong sense of his own self-worth or self-pride is going to have a difficult time trying to be a well-adjusted slave, since he will be in a constant state of conflict between what he needs and what society thinks of him. The best advice to give to such a person is to find one or more fellow wannabe slaves or one or more already slaves to give him the courage to say "to hell with society's judgment of me."

Chapter 26

Asking for the Opinion of a Slave

Every slave has a mind of his own, and the Master may call upon it in deciding what to do and what not to do with regards to events that affect one or both of them. However, such an opinion must be asked for or offered in such a way that it still sounds like the Master has the final decision on the matter. Thus, the Master may say, "Slave, if I gave you the choice, what would you (like to) do?" or "Slave, if you were your Master, what do you think he would do?" Never "What should I/we do?"

If it is the slave who really feels he needs to take the lead in offering an opinion, it can be done as, "Sir! May this slave offer an opinion on this matter?" or even more boldly, "Sir! If this slave were given a choice in this matter, he would …" Rare is the Master who is so self-centered or tyrannical as to not want input from the slave—especially on serious matters that affect them both. Not to ask for and accept such input is a good way of losing a slave.

Sometimes a slave has a view that is contrary to the Master's but still feels he must express it. He can do so as, "Sir! The humble experience of this slave has led him to a contrary view." If the Master does not wish to hear more, he will inform the slave of that, and technically that is the end of it. However, the skillful slave may be able to find some roundabout way to make his opinion heard.

Although silence on the part of a slave is ideal, sometimes the slave feels he must voice his opinion. This author was once involved in a leather discussion in which there were both Masters and slaves, and everyone was expected to participate. I was not "Mastered" at the time, so I was freer to speak than I would have otherwise. At one point, the issue came down to a certain Master's opinion versus mine. The Master was aggressively trying to challenge my opinion, and having felt that I had fully presented the facts as I believed them to be, I felt a need not to give in to him. However, rather than attempting to defend my position more aggressively by getting into an argument with the Master, I pulled out the proper slave card: "Sir! This slave has presented the situation as he sees it and stands by that. As a slave, it is inappropriate for me to get into an argument over this with a Master such as yourself; therefore, I must say no more on the issue, Sir!" A slave's position is never to get caught up in defense of his ego (I'm right, he's wrong).

The most significant opinion issue I had with a former Master was on who I was going to vote for. He came from a long line of Republicans. I was (and still am) a Democrat and had no intention of changing. Reminding me that the M/s relationship was not a democracy but a dictatorship, he ordered me to vote Republican. When I voted Democrat, which he knew I would, I told him and accepted the due punishment for having disobeyed.

Finally, many slaves are highly intelligent individuals, and as much as a slave may be expected to suppress any personal opinions, this can become a serious problem for any slave who requires intellectual stimulation within an M/s relationship.

Chapter 27

Slave Identity Drift (SID)

This may occur when a slave is not with his Master for a certain period of time. It is not that he starts to feel like a free person but that his sense of submissiveness weakens, and this can be depressing for him. SID can happen after only a few hours, such as being away from one's Master while at work, but this can usually be taken care of by a mid-work call or email to the Master. On days in which one is not in physical contact with the Master, such as if one of you needs to travel for work, then both a morning and evening phone/email contact can help. SID can be especially bad if one is in between Masters. In this case, the slave should try to wear his collar as much as possible and touch it often. He should try to avoid non-slave clothing as much as possible. He should seek slave friends or a slave rap group if possible. Although hooking up with a one-night stand or a weekend Dom will not relieve SID entirely, it may help significantly, especially if you have a sympathetic Dom who will "play" Master for you.

Chapter 28

Safe Sex vs. Bodily-Fluid Exchange

While there may be any number of unsafe sexual practices that do not involve bodily-fluid exchange, such as the use of drugs, here we will deal exclusively with only fluid exchange.

No Master should think that just because a person wants to submit to him that he has the right to subject the submissive to unsafe sex. Equally important, no submissive should think that to fulfill his submissive desires, he has to allow for, much less volunteer for, unsafe sex. The pure pleasure that a Master and slave should get from each other within safe sex ought to be more than enough of a hype to satisfy both of them, and if it does not, there is something wrong with the relationship.

The fluids in question can include saliva, urine, semen, blood, and feces. The exchange can be from the Master to the slave, the slave to the Master, or mutual. In the world of AIDS and more standard venereal diseases, especially those that either have no cure or are becoming resistant to antibiotics, most fluid exchange is bad news and to be avoided as much as possible.

Going from the safest to the most dangerous, we begin with saliva. Saliva is almost always safe unless one partner has a seriously diseased mouth. However, one takes a chance if one licks the skin of a recently flogged person, since at least micro-breaks and hence blood on the skin may be present. Some authorities have also warned against brushing one's teeth too soon before an intense exchange of saliva as the brush may also leave micro-cuts on the gums.

The issue of urine as part of the ritual of ownership is safe, as long as it is only in contact with the "uncompromised" surface of the skin (on no cuts or bruises), as might occur during a flogging; as long as it is not ingested, it is more or less safe. Otherwise, despite the common assumption that urine is germ-free, it is not. Certain infectious organisms can survive in it. So, unless one is absolutely sure that the urine is infection-free, (a difficult judgment to make), avoiding getting another person's urine in your face (mouth, nose, eyes) is always the best policy; however, one is immune to one's own urine, so being required to taste it, while usually unpleasant, is safe.

No part of the body should be pissed on that had recently been spanked, belted, caned, or flogged. This is a safety issue, in that there is always the possibility that the hitting of the skin has resulted in skin breaks that could then be contaminated by foreign urine.

This leaves us with the popular fluid-exchange substance: semen. In oral sex without a condom, even if the orgasm is not completed in the mouth, much less the semen swallowed, some degree of semen entering the mouth can still expose oral tissue to possible disease. All the above having been said, many people will take their chances; this is especially true in a Master/slave tradition that regards the semen of the Master to be such a part of the Master's self that for the slave to disrespect his semen by wasting it is to disrespect the Master.

In anal sex, this respect is sometimes given by the slave allowing for the Master to simply bareback the slave. I have found this to be most true for butt slaves—those slaves whose Masters are only into anal intercourse with their slaves, never oral sex.[89] In other cases, the slave accepts his Master's cum orally (without using a condom), but the Master always uses a condom for anal sex. This is based on the belief held by many that semen in the mouth is safer than semen in the rectum. Still, some Masters believe that absorption of the Master's semen into the slave's body is further proof of the Master's ownership of the slave, which may demand barebacking. However, there is a somewhat safer alternative, which is condom draining.

---

[89] A butt slave is not to be confused with a belly slave (the Master only fucks with his slave face down) or a back slave (with his face up).

Here the contents of the condom are drained into the mouth of the one who was fucked or even the fucker.

That some players might find this erotic should be not be difficult to figure out. When the condom is used and just thrown away, there is no eroticism directed to the condom itself. But condom draining can change that, whether the condom was in a mouth or up an asshole.

In a Master/slave relationship, the Master, to further prove his dominance (authority sex)[90] over the sub/slave, might require the sub/slave ingest the Dom/Master's semen, either before or after the sub/slave has been allowed to ejaculate. This is obviously an act of empowering erotic humiliation, and to intensify the humiliation, the Master may not only condom-fuck the slave and then drain the Master's semen into the mouth of the slave, but also may drop the condom into the slave's mouth, thereby requiring the slave to suck his own anal fluid off the condom. A modified version of this is when the Master empties his own semen into his own mouth and then transfers it into the mouth of the slave, who swallows it.

This brings us to the issue of felching or orally sucking semen out of the anus of one's partner.[91] This may be followed by the sucker, rather than swallowing, transferring cum to the mouth of the person he sucked it out of (who then swallows his own cum). The danger of this practice is obvious. This not only requires barebacking but the ingestion of foreign fecal material.

While most players are aware of the dangers of unprotected anal (fucking) and oral (sucking) sex, fewer are aware of the dangers of unprotected oral-anal (anilingus or analingus) sex; also known as a rim-job or rimming. In this, there is kissing, sucking, licking, and tonguing the anal opening, which presents a risk for getting or spreading any number of sexually transmitted infections (STIs) such as herpes, gonorrhea, human papillomavirus (HPV), hepatitis, and intestinal parasites that can infect the anus. It is also possible to be exposed to blood if there are cuts or tears in the anus or any traces of bloody feces. While a good washing can help remove a lot of potentially infectious material, it will not necessarily rid the area totally of such, and one takes his chances with this highly erotic

[90] See Chapter 23. Punishment.
[91] The act of sucking semen out of a vagina is known as cream-pie eating.

activity. Washing off with a disinfectant is probably better, but not likely, as no one wants to taste that on any part of the body. However, one guy the author played with who was really into rimming kept a jar of old beer and a cloth next to his bed and would insist on wiping off his and his playmate's anuses with it. Whether there was sufficient alcohol in the beer to do any good is open to question, but at least it did clean off the surface to some degree. In another case, an M/s couple were required by the contract that after each toileting that the Master and the slave had to wash off with antibacterial soap because both were into rimming each other. Another relatively safe way is to confine rimming to when one is mutually showering, so the players can get soap well into the rectum with their fingers. Of course, the safest oral/anal method is to use a latex barrier, with a dab of lube on the side covering the anus, as this can protect both partners.

The danger of blood, as in blood sports, is clear enough to most players to keep them away from it; however, there is always going to be that tiny group that will take the chance. For these I have no advice. However, the presence of blood is not always obvious, and a player who is not necessarily into blood may inadvertently come into contact with it. My own experience has been during flogging scenes. Even if there is no intention to draw blood, it can easily happen, and that blood can splatter into the face of the flogger.

For the Dom or Master who, with the consent of the sub or slave, is going to flog to the point of cutting (drawing blood), it is advisable for him to wear goggles. Blood landing on the mouth, nostrils, or worse, the eyes is never desirable; while goggles may not be erotic, a pragmatic Dom or Master should understand that safety comes first. Even less noticeable is the microscopic amounts of blood that can seep out of the skin, and should the flogger kiss, much less lick, a recently flogged back, a common act, a tiny ingestion of blood can occur.

The danger of feces (scat) is so obvious and well known that I know of no safe method of dealing with it.

Unprotected sex is always going to be a major issue in any sexual relationship, especially if the partners are not absolutely monogamous. For this reason, the issue of fluid exchange should be part of every M/s contract. For example, even if absolute monogamy is not acceptable, the contract may at least require "body-fluid monogamy," in which the Master and slave agree that any outside sexual activity would not include any fluid exchange. This is also referred to as "body-fluid bonding."

Naturally, such monogamy will work best if it is with one Master and one slave, but in a family with two or more slaves or a pair of Masters with one or more slaves, the chances of such limited fluid exchange is greatly reduced. Do the slaves only exchange only with the Master, or do they also exchange with each other?

Chapter 29

Outside Sexual Activity

The majority of Masters expect their slaves to have sex with them alone as either two-way (slave and Master) monogamy, or just one-way (slave alone) monogamy; but some Master/slave relationships are more open. This openness is of two general types. In the first, it is the Master who has full control of whom the slave will be allowed to have sex with, while the second (rarer) permits the slave to more or less freely choose his outside partners.

The first type requires planning on the part of the Master. The Master does not want to allow the slave to have sex with someone that the slave might find too desirable, but at the same time, the Master does not want to make the slave feel he is being punished by lending him out to an ogre. Of course, just such a choice does fall under the category of punishments a Master might inflict on a really naughty slave. The best way, therefore, to handle this type of outside sexual activity is for the Master and slave to come to a mutually acceptable compromise between too desirable and totally undesirable.

One might wonder why any Master would contractually agree to have a slave involved in outside sexual activity. The most common reason is to remind the slave that he is owned and his Master has the limited-by-contract right to offer his property to another Master, Dom, or just Top.

A second type of outside sexual activity is fraught with more dangers for both the Master and slave, in that either might find a partner more desirable than the present one, with the result that the latter is dumped. In this more promiscuous type of outside activity, the Master may not feel he can justify his own promiscuity without allowing the same for the slave. In this case, the Master is usually willing to take the chance because he is totally confident that he is the only right Master to his slave.

A form of semi-outside activity would be at something like a Master/slave trading party. Here, several pairs of Master/slaves (best four to six)[92] get together, and each Master plays with one or more slaves other than his own. Since the Master of a slave is still present, it is not a full tricking out. Naturally, this only works if the Masters and slaves know each other well.

When it comes to the slave having the freedom to trick out, some Masters prefer to still retain some control over the slave's behavior, which usually means the Master insists that the slave follows certain rules. These rules may serve three purposes: (1) They remind the slave that he is still under the Master's authority. (2) They force the slave to admit to the trick that the slave has a Master, even if that Master is not present. (3) More often than not, they are intended to reduce the chances of the slave actually hooking up with a trick.

With regards to number three, I will give two examples from my own so-called freedom to trick out. In both cases, I was allowed that freedom only if the Master and I were away from each other for a week or more.

In the first example, the Master insisted that before I went home with a trick, I had to read the following limitations to the prospective trick:

"This slave has his Master's permission to trick out, however only under the following circumstances. He is only permitted to take his Master's cock cream in his mouth or allow his Master to shove his unsheathed shaft up this slave's asshole; a condom for both sucking and getting fucked is otherwise required. If rimming is demanded, this slave must first wash off the asshole to be tongued. If he is to be bitten, as on the back of his neck or butt, the biter's teeth may not break the skin. If pissed on, since only the Master can shoot into this slave's mouth or on his clothes, it is only below the neck and while naked that this slave can be so baptized by another. Also, if he is to be flogged, the pissing must come before that, not

---

[92] Fewer than four is not enough variety, and more than six becomes difficult to manage.

after.[93] As for any flogging, while it would normally be with the Master's toy, for anyone else it would be with this slave's. Also, if this slave is to be pushed around or otherwise strongly manhandled, it cannot be in any way that would damage his body. Since even this slave's Master in his most forceful punishment of this slave never does anything this slave would regard as abusive, no one else may abuse this slave. Finally, if the slave is to be handcuffed, it is only in the front, since only his Master or a familiar Dom may cuff him behind, and it's either the slave's cuffs that would be used or the slave needs to see the key to any other cuffs."

The Master believed that this listing of serious play would frighten off some prospective tricks, although he also understood that it could actually turn other tricks on, especially those who had never tricked with a slave before and found it exciting.

The second example of a Master who allowed for outside tricking had a different approach to restricting rules. I could never expose more of my flesh than was absolutely necessary for the sexual act. If I was getting a blow job, I was to unzip, pull out my dick only to the degree I might when needing to pee, but never unbuckle my pants or push them down. If I was getting fucked, I could unzip, unbuckle, and push the back of the pants down to expose my bare butt, but no more than the minimum I would need to if I were sitting on a toilet; and furthermore, the guy behind me was not allowed to touch my dick. It was front work or back work, never both. Also, in either case, my feet had to remain on the ground. Naturally, this limited my tricking-out possibilities to little more than standing-up quickies, usually in a back room or restroom with a lockable door. The whole point of these restrictions was the Master's way of limiting the amount of access another person had to my body and thus to remind me that I could only be fully naked when serving him. In short, his rules were like permitting me candy while making it difficult to eat.

Actually, a Master does not need to justify his outside sexual activity, as long as it does not threaten the health and safety of the slave or deny the slave his sexual due from the Master. Nonetheless, one of my short-term Masters was so anti-monogamous that he felt it was only fair that the

---

[93] Flogging may cause tiny cuts in the skin which, if exposed to urine, could be unsafe. See Chapter 54. Floggers.

slave have equal sexual freedom, but to remind the slave that this was a gift, not a right, the slave would have to pay for that gift. This meant that if one of us did trick out, he was contractually obligated to tell the other, after which the slave was to be punished. Yes! The slave was punished not only for his permitted infidelity, but also for the Master infidelity.[94] The Master's motto was "When we cheat, the slave I must beat." After all, he was the Master, hence the one who had the inherent right to trick out; the slave had no such inherent right.

What is important to note here was that this punishment for the Master's wrongdoings, while seemingly unfair, was clearly stated in the contract. For just getting sucked off, there was no penalty. The least penalty was if either gave a blow job to someone else; the next was if either fucked someone else; the third was if either sucked off and fucked someone; and the worst penalty was getting fucked by someone else.

For the worst offense, the punishment usually consisted of some version of "authority sex"—where the slave either milks himself or is milked by the Master to de-eroticize the slave, after which there would be sexual demands made on the less sexually interested slave, which could include a non-erotic flogging. In other words, it was sex mainly to establish the Master's slightly sadistic authority over the slave. Obviously, this was another example of the power games Masters play.

Many Masters choose to grow into monogamy with their slave. The Master and slave, for the first few months, may be allowed one or two outside partners a month, then only every other month, then only once or twice the first year, with full monogamy from then on.

---

[94] See Chapter 23. Punishment.

Chapter 30

Bondage and Other Bodily Restrictions and Safety

Bondage, which includes mummification, is a popular erotic activity, but it also has it risks. *Bondage* here refers to the practice of a submissive offering himself for total surrender to the Dominant through immobilization with rope or chains, or more intensely through mummification. For those who are not into such bondage scenes, being immobilized may seem a very unsafe condition, but for many into bondage, it gives them a deep sense of security and safety. The first rule is to never have an amateur put anyone into bondage. Rope or chains can cut off circulation and interfere with breathing. Also, bondage of any kind may be difficult to get out of in case of an emergency. Those who are well-trained in bondage know this and make sure they have the proper means of freeing a submissive rapidly.

Although bondage and discipline (D) are sometimes distinguished from sadomasochism (SM), the two cross over a lot. While most bondage is not done with the intention of stimulation pain itself, some of it is. In other cases, bondage is only auxiliary to SM. Here, a sub who is undergoing the pleasures of pain might thrash around and in such a sudden and unexpected movement, he might cause the Dom to unintentionally cause harm to the sub. For this reason, it is often best to limit the sub's ability to move, even if the sub is not primarily turned on to bondage. Still, in other bondage scenes, the goal is sensory deprivation and whatever follows it.

The most dangerous form of (sensory-deprivation) bondage is full mummification, because the mummy (especially a first-timer) may quickly panic in such total constraint. Also, dehydration due to excessive sweating, and hyperthermia followed by hypothermia (once unmummified) are risks. This kind of bondage can also send the mummy into an altered state of consciousness, which may make him incapable of realizing that his body is under too much distress, which is why he must never be left alone. In fact, for safety reasons, the mummy should always have at least two mummifiers present, in case the mummy, for whatever reason, needs to be unmummified in a hurry.

The need for a second person or assistant mummifier is absolutely imperative if mummification is to turn from bondage into cocooning. This is mummification specifically to cause the mummy to enter into a sensory-deprived altered state of consciousness, where he will meet his inner gods and demons, and because of possible psychological trauma, the persons in charge of the mummy should be prepared to unmummify him at a moment's notice.

Although not strictly bondage, three related items come under the safety issue. A sub or slave should never let an unfamiliar or not-fully-trusted Dominant put him in a cage. Nor should the sub allow himself to be handcuffed by a stranger. For the slave who insists on taking this risk, he should at least only permit it with his hands in front, not behind him. This way he has some control over his own safety.

A slave should also be cautious with any unfamiliar Dominant who wants to put the slave in bondage and then gag him. Many Masters like to gag their slaves during play or even as a punishment to a verbal offense, but no slave should ever have a gag in his mouth that he cannot remove by himself in an emergency or if the Dom goes too far and the sub needs to start screaming. Another danger, rare as it may be, is if the Dom suddenly had a heart attack and the bottom could not call out for help due to having a gag he could not remove.

Finally, a responsible Dominant always asks a submissive if he has any breathing problem (such as asthma) before putting any gag into the sub's mouth that may interfere in his breathing through his mouth. Remember that the world is divided up into those who breathe primarily through the nose and those who breathe primarily through the mouth (like me). On the other hand, a gag that simply prevents a submissive from talking need not interfere with his breathing. Remember that in the kinky sex Scene, safe sex does not just mean condoms; it means knowing your playmate's health issues.

Chapter 31

Silent Alarm Partner

There is always the danger, even in a vanilla bar, of going home with a stranger; but considering some of the games leather people play, it is especially recommended that you notify a friend who can be your silent alarm partner (SAP), presumably one into the Scene, about where and with whom you are going for such play. This situation should technically not arise for a slave who has a Master but could arise for an unattached slave looking for a Master. An SAP might also be needed by a slave who has some freedom to trick out.

One does not bring up the issue of an SAP unless the scene goes wrong and one's playmate refuses to stop it. At that point, you should not just tell him you have notified your SAP but direct him to your wallet, where he can find a piece of paper or a card that says in big, bold letters *Silent Alarm Partner,* followed by one—or better, two or three—phone numbers. If this doesn't work, start screaming in the hope of waking up some neighbors. This last resort is a major reason you should never allow a gag to be put into your mouth by an unfamiliar player.

Chapter 32

Safe Word

A safe word is one used in sadomasochistic sexual practices to indicate that a participant (bottom) is having a problem with the scene and may want it to stop. In some SM scenes, there may be three levels of safe words. Level I, "Please Sir! Check in with me, as something is not quite right." Level II, "Sir! Something is seriously wrong, and if it is not fixed, the scene is going to have to end immediately." Level III, "I have had all I can take, and the scene must come to an end, at least for now." Any safe word should be something the bottom would not normally say in either a scene or non-scene situation. For example: "Dungeon dinosaur." Some SM and M/s players use a different safe word for each level. For example, traffic lights, whereby if the Master asks if the slave is all right, the slave might say "Green," which means "Yes. Continue." The slave may also say, with or with the master asking, "Yellow," to indicate the scene needs to be lightened up or slowed down or stopped for a while; "Orange" to indicate getting close to the slave's limit; and "Red," the limit has been reached, and it is time to stop altogether.

Remember: if one is signing a contract, the exact form or forms of the safe word(s) should be in the contract.

Chapter 33

Going Feral

This describes a situation in which a submissive in an SM scene enters a dangerous atavistic or animalistic state of consciousness, in which the submissive can do serious harm to himself or others around him. Remember that during an SM scene, the players are playing as much or more with one another's minds as with their bodies. Intense SM activities can send the bottom and/or the Top into altered states of consciousness (ASC), which automatically will cloud judgments. If alcohol or drugs are added to the scene, a dangerous situation is guaranteed. In other words, "safe and sane" automatically means "no drugs."

Going feral is very rare outside extreme or edge-playing scenes, that is a scene in which there is a potential danger to one or more of the players' health, physical safety, or even life; in other words, during risk-aware consensual kink (RACK). This is in contrast to SSC (safe, sane, and consensual). Some feral goers can actually harm themselves if put into restraints, but if they are already in them, it may be too dangerous to themselves or the Dom to release them. Some extreme edge players are known as kamikaze (willing to risk all), but these are not respected in the general SM community.

Since one person's edge play is simply another person's heavy but normal play, what is and is not edge play is difficult to judge. However, in any scene where the submissive may actually feel his safety or life is under threat, there is the possibility for a very primal (feral) response arising.

Among the activities that could most likely lead to a feral response are the use of knives, electricity, and fire play.[95]

Obviously, the best way to avoid this is to avoid edge play, but for those into such play, this is not always possible. However, there are some precautions players can take. A Dominant should never enter into an edge play with a sub he has not played with before in some less extreme way, because that sub may not feel sufficiently safe. Even if an edge-playing Dom knows that an edge-playing sub has never gone feral with other edge-playing Doms, that is no guarantee that it will not happen with him. The relationship between every Dom and sub is unique, and even if they have edge played before, every new scene is also unique. This is because what went on in the players' lives, even only hours before the scene, can dramatically alter the players' subconscious reaction to a scene that may have been played out before. Also, as mentioned above, while alcohol and drugs should be excluded from all SM scenes, this is doubly true for edge players.

With the exception of mummification, I have consistently refused to be an edge player, either as a Dom or sub. Therefore, I have never had to deal with a feral player, and so the best advice I have been given by those who are in the know is if it happens, try to keep the feral sub as restrained as is safely possible, to calm him down, and if necessary call for help. That help can best be assured if there is a third player on hand.

---

[95] Since unlike whips and bondage, these are not so closely associated with the slavery issue, I will not mention them further.

Chapter 34

Aftercare[96]

Unlike most vanilla sexual activities, any intense B/D, SM, D/s, or M/s sexual scene should require that the players do more than one or both getting dressed and leaving or both players just going to bed. An aftercare of some kind should occur. This can be as simple as the Dominant cuddling the submissive or talking to the submissive to show that he cares about the sub he may just have worked over. In a full M/s relationship, this aftercare is even more important to demonstrate to the slave that whatever the Master has put him through is valued by the Master.

Kinky sex, especially if it involves pain, is more than what happens to the body; it is what is going on in the deepest parts of the minds of both players. Thus, after any intense scene, it must be asked, "Have the invisible minds, as well as the visible body, of the players, come through safely?"

Unfortunately, some slaves feel it is not their place to make aftercare demands on the Master; however, if the Master is unaware of the slave's need, he cannot be expected to help. But every slave needs to be aware that a Master may have played with other slaves who have shown little or no need for much aftercare, so the Master may be unaware of such a need. Once made aware of the slave's need, if the Master is unwilling to supply this, then the Master is inadequate. The need for a proactive approach by the slave on this issue is even greater if the slave does not live with the

---

[96] Sometimes spelled as after care.

Master and experiences a delayed slave-drop (depression), since there may be no Master around to help with it.[97]

Because of the intense emotional level that usually exists between a slave and his Master, a slave can easily over-identify with a Master. If this happens, and there comes a point when the slave feels that the Master is withdrawing from him, this can lead to feelings of depression or separation anxiety. The most obvious point at which this can happen is right after an intense sexual experience when the Master, perhaps feeling tired, assumes the slave needs no further attention, no aftercare, and more or less leaves the slave to his own devices. The slave, feeling he has received too little feedback, may enter into a state of self-doubt. This can be specific self-doubt as in, "Did I fail to please this Master sufficiently?" It can also be more general self-doubt as in, "Is there something wrong with wanting or trying to be a slave?" Such self-doubt may be exaggerated when the emotional and sexual high and loss of self the slave may have been feeling disappears and is replaced by a letdown of ordinary or normal self-awareness. The slave may tell himself that this is irrational thinking, but that may make matters worse, since now he may wonder about his own sanity.

Sometimes this "slave drop" may not occur immediately but a day or even two days later, but whether it is immediate or delayed, the slave should recognize it as a common part of being a slave and know that he must not wait passively for the Master to supply confidence-building, doubt-dispelling aftercare, but actively seek it out.[98]

While some slaves need a lot of aftercare, others need only a little, and some seem to need none, but they are rare. Also, the degree of aftercare may depend on the type of scene; therefore, when a Master and slave are still in the negotiation stage, one of the items carefully and honestly discussed should be aftercare.

Aftercare can actually have a hidden benefit to it. It is a natural point for a Master and slave to do some healthy/healing interchange without threatening the Master's authority. As the Master is working to let the slave

---

[97] I have been very lucky not to have had any serious slave (sub)-drop, and most of my information on it comes from Kim Debron, who can be reached at Kimdebron. com. See "Maintaining an M/s Relationship."

[98] See below for "Top-drop."

know just how valuable the slave is, the Master may wish to prove this by asking the slave if there is something the Master can do to reward the slave. This can give the slave an indirect sense of power over the Master, and the secure Master can take advantage of this to partially leave his often-exhausting status as the one always in charge. In other words, it can help reduce status exhaustion or burnout of both the slave and the Master.[99]

One Master/slave couple I knew used this aftercare time for play reversal when the Master, who liked getting fucked, would as an aftercare reward allow his slave, who like to fuck, to fuck the Master.

---

[99] See Chapter 43. Maintaining the M/s Relationship.

Chapter 35

Family Situations

The Master must always respect the family situation of the slave and vice versa. This can be a problem, in that the average family, even one that is supportive of a gay relationship, may have trouble dealing with the very concept of a Master/slave relationship, in which case it may be necessary to keep the specifics of that relationship hidden (in the closet) or at least considerably downplayed. This can naturally create tension in the relationship, which should not simply be dismissed or otherwise left undealt with. Any time a Master and slave must pretend to have a non-dominant/submissive relationship, there is an automatic disruption in that relationship. If this is not repaired, it could lead to more serious problems. Even the shortest such disruptions require repairing, and some special action or extra effort should be employed as soon as possible to reestablish the dominant/submissive status.

Some Masters try to deal with this by having the slave give up his family for the relationship, but any Master who does so is an insecure control freak and is not going to make for an adequate Master for any slave. If the slave's family situation is in such conflict with the Master/slave relationship that even being closeted about it is not working, then the slave may have to abandon his family, but this must be entirely up to the slave with the Master remaining totally neutral. Naturally, the situation can be in the reverse, with the Master's family having a problem with such a relationship. Here again, it is the Master who must deal with it while slaves remain neutral.

Chapter 36

Former Friends

When a slave finds a Master, especially for the first time, he may discover that it affects his relationships with many, if not most, of his friends. This is less so if his friends are in the leather or kinky community and will probably be able to integrate themselves into the new M/s relationship. Those outside the community, even if they are sympathetic to the M/s relationship, may have a much more difficult time with that relationship. Actually, this may not be too much different from what happens when a wife and husband get married; one or both individuals will lose contact with some friends and develop new contacts. The difference is that it is more likely that due to the demands of the Master, the slave will be the one to lose some friends, while the Master may not lose any. But this is not an excuse for any Master to purposely try, much less demand, the slave give up friends so that the Master can isolate the new slave from all but himself. Only a very insecure Master will try this. One way such a Master will try to do this is to forbid the slave from phoning or emailing other people without first clearing it with him. A slave might want it to be put into the contract that he has the right to free access to friends, especially if the slave is being required to reside in the Master's home.

Chapter 37

Outside Work

In almost all cases, a Master and slave will have normal jobs, independent of the Master/slave relationship, and if the relationship is to be successful, it should not interfere with those jobs. Since the average employer, even one that is tolerant of gay employees, may have trouble dealing with the very concept of a Master/slave relationship, then like the family issue above, it may be necessary to keep that relationship hidden (in the closet).

Regardless of how hidden or open the M/s relationship is to the outside, the fact is that the slave, unless self-employed, will have an authority over him (his boss) that competes with that of the Master's authority over him. As in any serious interference with the Master's status, there must be some special action or extra effort to reestablish the dominant/submissive status, this time on a daily basis. This can be as simple as kneeling at the Master's feet while the collar he would not likely be wearing at work is put back on him by the Master and then having the slave kiss and lick the boots, shoes, or bare feet of the Master.[100] If such an authority reestablishing ritual is not done, it will almost certainly lead to a weakening of the relationship. Always remember the exact nature of any action or effort to counter outside work authority should be properly delineated in the Master/slave contract.

In most cases, the outside job will not be a serious problem, provided

---

[100] The slave might lick the boots and feet of any Master he is playing with, but he only kisses those of his own contracted Master. He likewise only kisses the hand of his own, not another, Master.

the sphere of the two jobs does not overlap, or worse the Master and slave are employed by the same employer. This could become a very serious problem if the slave's position is superior to that of the Master. This naturally creates tension in the relationship, which must be reduced as soon as possible. In the one such employment case of this kind I knew of, the slave (boss at work) was required to go through the "pissed-on ownership ritual" Monday through Friday at home.

One major concern with outside work is that the Master or slave may bring his job problems home with him. This is less of an issue if the Master does it, because the slave is expected to accept this burden imposed on him. But the Master is not expected to have the slave burden him with the slave's problems. To deal with this naturally unequal situation will require great skill on the part of the Master. This can be done within the authority set up between the two if the Master takes the lead. If the Master senses that the slave's outside day has been rough, he can order the slave to tell him about it, in short, to vent, and then order the slave to take what time he needs to calm down and remain out of service until he does so. This show of support by the Master should go a long way in making the slave feel that the Master cares enough to even release him temporarily from any further burden. This may well help the slave want to double his service to his thoughtful Master.

Chapter 38

Finances

It is the assumption of many Masters that a slave should not only turn over his paycheck to the Master but all other financial resources the slave has. This can work well if the slave has very few such resources, which is the usual case, but not so well if the slave has anything substantial and/or has more than the Master. Naturally, this can be a dangerous setup for financial exploitation, especially if the slave earns more money than the Master. In this case, in a number of contracts between a slave and Master, there will be clauses such as: (a) There will be no interference by the Master with regards to the slave's outside employment, and (b) The finances of the Master and slave will in no way be mixed. The Master's savings and debts are his alone, as those of the slave are his.

Such clauses are especially important in those contracts under a year-long in duration. However, even in many longer-term contracts, it is clearly stated that the slave's finances remain independent of those of the Master and vice versa. This is one reason why any contract that has any potentially exploitive clause should be signed by four witnesses. In this way, should the slave decide to leave the Master, that Master cannot rightly be accused by an angry former slave of involuntary financial exploitation or outright theft.

Also, a good reason for keeping their finances separate is that should the relationship go bad, the slave may feel trapped in the relationship because he has lost control over his own money. For this reason, some slaves keep a known or secret "freedom" or "to-hell-with-you" fund, which can be used if the M/s relationship suddenly breaks up, with the slave having no other resources to leave the relationship with.

Exploitation, however, can go the other way, with a financially incompetent slave trying to live off of a foolish Master. The fact is that very few Masters have the resources to house, feed, clothe, and otherwise take full responsibility for a slave, not to mention any medical care the slave may at some point need. Finally, being a slave who does not have an outside or taxable income does not do well when he is no longer young.

Chapter 39

Property of the Slave

Obviously, slaves come to a Master with some degree of personal property. In most cases, this is more than just the clothes on their bodies. It will often include a car and may include household goods or even a house itself. This should mean that these items have to be part of any contractual negotiations. Naturally, a house or condominium in particular may be a problem. Personal property gives a slave a certain amount of freedom that some Masters will object to and require the slave to either sell or turn over to the Master. This, of course, is open to potential financial exploitation of the slave. Other Masters will tolerate such personal property but may insist that once the contract is signed, any new acquisition of property be approved by the Master.

Chapter 40

Religious or Spiritual Practice

No Master should ever interfere with the right of the slave to practice his or her religious or spiritual tradition. In fact, if a Master finds that practice either distasteful or as incompatible with his relationship with his slave, then he needs a different slave. This must be put into the contract.

Chapter 41

Finding a Master, Finding a Slave

Before a Master starts looking for a slave, he should be very sure of what he wants from that slave. Equally, before a slave goes looking for a Master, he should be sure of what way he is willing to serve that Master. This means that a long-term Master/slave relationship, first of all, will depend on a match between the slave and Master, and this is often complicated by the fact that there are a lot of pseudo-Masters and pseudo-slaves out there. Some know they are phonies, while others do not. These pseudo-Masters and pseudo-slaves will soon show what they really are by rapidly disappointing any authentic opposite, and one will soon dump the other.

Every slave starts out as a wannabe, but only a few wannabes ever become slaves, and it is the job of the Master to separate one from the other.

My personal experience has been with three different Masters who each responded in their own unique way to me. One Master was not into spending any time on the uninitiated and so told the wannabe about resources he could turn to. Such a Master is not likely to be a very good trainer.

A second Master decided on an intimate or hands-on approach. He invited the wannabe home, instructed the wannabe in the standard slave position, and then ordered the wannabe to strip in front of the Master, kneel, and beg the Master to give the wannabe a chore to do. The Master gave him an easy one that was finished in no more than half an hour, all the time being watched by the Master. The Master, satisfied with the wannabe's completion, dismissed the wannabe with the order to return at a given time and day. If the wannabe expected to have hot sex in this "testing," he was left frustrated or experiencing the discipline of denial. In this case, the wannabe was sincere and returned. The Master required the wannabe to refer to himself only as a wannabe (slave) until the Master felt he had earned the right to be referred to as a boy, gamma (slave in training), or just slave.

A third Master took what I regarded as the most professional approach. Over a series of days and emails, the Master established an extensive dialog with the wannabe to establish what category the potential slave was in,[101] what the slave candidate knew or thought he knew about becoming a slave, and what that wannabe might and might not have in common with the Master, both in the vanilla world and the SM world.

It is a common occurrence that a Master type and slave type first meet in a kinky situation and become so sure that they are kink compatible that they rush into a relationship, only to discover that outside of the kink they are a terrible match. Also, remember that something might be compatible if the two of you were in a vanilla relationship that might not be compatible in an M/s relationship. For example, two people of very different educational backgrounds might work in vanilla, but automatically the more educated means the higher the status, the less educated means the lower the status, so while in an M/s situation a Master who is more educated than his slave may work, a slave more educated than the Master will almost certainly result in problems. So, both potential Master and slave should not only look deeply into each other's background, but how that will work out in the long run.

Several Masters I have known have told me that the best way to interview a potential slave is to go from the most general to the more specific. The list of questions below assumes that the person interviewed is a wannabe slave, not someone who has been a slave. For the latter, many of these questions can be dropped. At the same time, a Master who has nothing to hide should be prepared to have the wannabe ask the Master many of the same questions in return.

Before getting into the questions, there is no doubt that hooking up with people has become easier than ever through the internet. However,

---

[101] See Chapter 5. Why Be a Slave?

a Master/slave hookup in that manner may be helpful for an initial introduction, but not for anything more than that. The truth is that real and phony Masters looking for slaves and real or phony slaves looking for Masters will lie. The obvious basic rule is to never give too much information about yourself on the internet until you have met the person face to face. To ignore this warning is asking for trouble and even danger. Accept no excuse for a face-to-face meeting. Especially do not accept "I live too far away right now to meet." If this is the case, then what is the use of the two even thinking about a relationship? Also, do not be seduced by a slowly developing internet fantasy M/s relationship. Distance has a safety about it that can become very unsafe when you start to believe that everything said is true. Fantasy is fantasy, and reality is reality; never forget that.

Once both parties have decided that they have mutual proof of sincerity, the interview can begin.

"Have you been a slave before?" If yes, "Tell me about the relationship" (and/or) "Would there be a problem in me asking him about you?" Counter question: "Sir! Have you had a slave before?"[102] If yes, "Sir! can you tell me about him/them?" (and/or) "Sir! Would there be a problem in me asking him about you?"

"Do you have any friends that you would feel comfortable in vouching for your character?" If a Master has the right to ask this of a wannabe, the wannabe has the right to ask this of a potential Master.

Assuming this is simply a wannabe slave, the questions might go as follows.

"What do you think a slave is?"[103] Chances are the wannabe has only the foggiest idea.

"What kind of slave do you imagine yourself to be?" This means a pet or sex slave, a worker or domestic slave, or a show slave, etc.[104]

"Do you know any slaves?" Chances are either no or maybe one. If he

---

[102] This is the same as asking, "Have you been a Master before?"

[103] This manual has consistently defined a slave as a submissive who will accept punishment of some kind or degree.

[104] This will require some explanation from the Master.

knows one, then the wannabe should explain how and where, but with full instructions to give no personal names.

"Why do you want to be a slave?" He'd better have a good answer. Once the wannabe answers this, he has every right to ask the Master why he is a Master, and he'd better have a good answer too.

"What do you think a Master is?" Chances are, the wannabe again has only the foggiest idea. And again, a potential slave should have the right to ask a potential Master the opposite question, and the Master who has not thought about this and answered this to himself in perhaps more than one way does not deserve to have a slave. The greatest fear of anyone who calls himself a Master should be that a potential slave concludes that the man interviewing him is a Master only because he calls himself a Master. In other words, can the Master show that he is acknowledged by his peers as a Master.

Assuming the dialog has not fallen apart, it may continue.

"Do you know the differences between a Daddy/boy, SM, Dom/sub, and Master/slave relationship?" Chances are, the wannabe is looking for one of the first three versus the last.

"Why do you think you might want me as a Master?"

"What do you think power exchange means in an M/s relationship?"

"What kind of past sexual relationships have you had?"

"What do you know about such terms as bondage and discipline; rimming; water sports; risk awareness consensual kick (RACK); safe, sane, and consensual; felching; fisting; cock and ball torture; and so forth?"[105]

"Do you understand that you would need to follow some degree of slave protocol even when not with the Master?" Chances are, a wannabe has little or no knowledge about slave protocol.

"Do you have any fears about being a slave?" The potential slave or even a former slave who says no is either lying or a fool.[106]

"What does the word *obedience* mean to you?"

"What do you think loyalty to a Master means?"

---

[105] Unless the Master is really into some of these activities or the potential slave has mentioned one or more of the latter, the Master might not want to ask about them, for concern about scaring the slave away.

[106] For a slave negotiating with a new potential Master, the slave should at least always fear that the he may not be able to live up to the expectations of the Master.

"Want do the words *discipline* and *punishment* mean to you?" Chances are, this will help scare off a few insincere wannabes.[107]

"What do you think you need to do to become a good slave?"

"What do you fantasize about when you masturbate?"

"Describe three M/s fantasies."

"Subtracting work, school, family obligations, etc., how much time would you have left to serve a Master?"

"Describe your relationship with friends, family, coworkers, even your boss." This is one of the questions to determine the kind of psychological baggage the wannabe might bring with him.

"Are you out as gay person or still closeted? If out, who are you out to?" If the Master as a gay person is still closeted, he is not going to want an out slave. If the Master is out, having a closeted slave could make for a very limited relationship. After all, if a person has to hide simply being gay in this "gay rights era," how much more is he going to be in the closet about his kink?

"Even if you are out as a gay person to family, friends, and coworkers, how do you think they would react if they found out that you were a slave?" While some M/s couples do everything they can to hide the M/s part of their relations, other couples find what works is that they start out pretending to be vanilla together, to get to know the other person's friends, family, coworkers, even boss if possible, and gradually reveal the deeper nature of their relationship.

"Are you looking for a closed or an open sexual relationship?"

"Have you ever been sexually abused?"

"Have you ever been abused non-sexually?"

"What are your ideas about safe sex?"

"Have you ever been in a three-way or an orgy?"

"Are you prone to jealousy?"

"What if the Master wants to have sex with others but wants you to be monogamous?"

---

[107] Remember, in this manual, *discipline* is erotic discipline, while *punishment* is nonerotic discipline. Some Masters may choose to ask this question further down the list, so as not to scare off a potential slave, but if it not asked within the first dozen or so questions, the Master may be wasting his time on the rest of the interview.

"What are your feelings about pornography?"

"What's your view on drag?"

"What sex toys do you own?"

"What are your feelings about romance or love outside of a M/s relationship versus within a M/s relationship?"

"On a one-to-five scale, what do you think your erotic pain tolerance is?" The Master is not really asking for a specified number so much as if the slave uses a low, medium, or high one.

"Do you smoke?"

"Have you ever had an alcohol problem?"

"Have you used any kind of drugs? If so which ones?"

"When was the last time you were depressed and why?" The Master should be less interested in anyone episode of depression, since almost everyone has occasion to be rightfully depressed. What the Master is fishing for is whether this slave candidate is prone to serious bouts of depression.

"Have you any particular medical issues?"

"How important is your health to you? Do you exercise, eat properly?" No Master wants a slave who, if he does not care for himself, will not care for the Master.

"Do you have medical and dental insurance?" Remember, few Master have enough resources to take care of the medical needs of a slave.

"Do you have any special dietary needs?"

"How clean and tidy do you keep your living quarters?" This should be especially important to a Master who wants a slave at least partially as a domestic.

"Do you have a pet and/or if the Master has a pet how would you feel about it?" My present Master had two cats when I met him, and I am allergic to cats, so my Master had to spend most of his time at my place or get rid of the cats, which neither of us wanted, since both of us were animal lovers.

"Have you had any legal problem and/or ever been arrested?"

"Where did you go to school, and what was your experience there?"

"How secure is your job?"

"How many jobs have you had in the past five years?"

"Do you consider yourself a financially responsible person?"

"Do you live within your income?"

"Do you have any debts?" A Master who chooses a slave with significant debts is either very rich or a fool. A Master has the right to require that a potential slave show him his billing and payment history. No slave should be a financial burden on his Master, which is why that Master has a right to control unnecessary purchases or acquisitions of a slave in accordance with the contract. A pre-contract slave who is asking for such information should have the right to see a potential Master's debt records.

"Do you understand the difference between needs and wants?"[108] None of us have many needs that cannot easily be taken care of, but we all have an unending number of wants. A slave must accept that while the Master must not deny the slave his needs, all the slave's wants are dependent entirely on his Master to allow or deny.[109]

"Do you consider yourself a patient person? This is to say someone who will need to wait at the Master's pleasure?"

"Do you have any hobbies or special interests?" A conflict in these could be made for any relationship. Too many outside interests may steal from the time the Master expects the slave to devote to him.

"What kind of music do you like?"

"What kind sports interest you?"

"What kind of movies, plays, or TV shows do you like?"

"What other kinds of nonsexual entertainment interest you?" (Museums, art shows, camping, etc.)

"Do you have any interest in politics?" If a Master has such interests, he might want a slave with such interests, or if the Master is apolitical, he may not want a slave who is political.

"Do you vote?" Yes to this shows a person with a sense of community responsibility.

"How skilled at a computer are you?"

"Do you consider yourself punctual, or do you make a habit of being

---

[108] See Chapter 45. Love and Romance.

[109] Needs are all the things that keep the slave alive, in health and safety, and optimally ready to serve his Master. Everything else is a want and should never be asked for by a slave directly. For some slaves, only needs are sufficient, while for other slaves, occasional wants may be granted them by their Masters as a reward for certain exceptional service. Also see Chapter 23. Punishment.

a little or a lot late?" A Master can pardon a lot, but being kept waiting or having things not done on time is a serious sin.

"Do you think of yourself as a person who makes a commitment or promise and keeps it?" To know this, you will have to have spent a good amount of pre-contract time with the person or grill the person's friends on this issue.

"If you had a chance to change any part of your body, what would you like to change?"

The Master should not be too specific here, because that will make the slave think the Master is likely to be critical of some part of the slave's body.

"Do you understand that you should not gain or lose weight, or have any voluntary bodily modifications without the Master's permission?" This will extend to any changes in hairstyle or color.

"What are three things in the M/s relationship that could alienate you?" Examples: (1) Asking to have control of my finances. (2) Having unsafe sex with another person. (3) Not respecting my pain limitations (abusing me).

"What do you know about me as a Master and non-Master?" The best slave would have checked you out, and if he did not, he is so new to the Scene that he does not know how, or is just naïve, or arrogantly feels he can figure you out on his own or worse, handle whatever you might throw at him. This usually means bad slave material and possibly an unsafe player.

"Is there something in particular you think you could bring to an M/s relationship other than what you think of as standard stuff?"

"Are you willing to keep a daily activity log or journal, especially of times when you are not with the Master and show it to him on demand?"

In summary of the above, the rule is to probe, probe, and probe ruthlessly and be suspicious about inconsistencies, half-truths, and lies.

I repeat: while the above list is technically directed at the prospective slave, there is every reason for the prospective slave to use these questions to find out if he thinks the Master is suitable for him.

It is highly advisable that the Master and slave spend at least a month together just learning about each other as whole persons before any contract is signed, because the greatest mistake either party can commit is to rush into an M/s relationship. In fact, both sides should be suspicious of any desire to rush things. A Master or slave who does not have the patience to wait at least a month before a contract is even negotiated is almost certain to be a poor Master or slave. During this time, the Master should check the ability of the wannabe slave to be silent; to avoid a constant use of the pronoun "I"; not to talk mainly about himself vs. others; not to be too talkative altogether; not to be easily offended by others; not to be too critical of others; not to disregard the opinion of others; and to check if the potential slave is subject to undesirable mood swings.

At the end of any interview like this, if the potential Master is satisfied with the potential slave's answers and the slave has not been scared away, the Master might assign one to three outside chores for the slave to perform, to check to see how well the slave obeys orders, wants to please the Master, and will follow through in a timely manner. The chore(s) should be totally nonsexual. After all, most of the slave's interactions with the Master are likely to be nonsexual unless they only interact for sex. Also, they should be something the slave would be reluctant to do otherwise.

One Master I knew had a prospective slave learn how to prepare a certain meal from scratch, even though the slave had no cooking skills. A second chore was for the slave to make up a detailed minimum budget for the next month and then prove to the Master how well he could live with it. A third was for a slave who had no interest in the Bible but who was assigned to read the first five books of it (the Torah) and write out a one-page double-spaced review of each book. Believe me, this was sadomasochistic torture for the poor slave.

While the above questionnaire is more for a wannabe slave, many of the questions can be used to interview even an experienced slave, and if so, the following additional questions should be asked. "Under what conditions did you separate from your former Master(s)? Have you had enough time to process that separation? Are you experiencing any slave identity drift?"[110]

Finally, make sure that both of you have a good sense of humor, so that when things go wrong that neither of you could have foreseen or avoided, you will both be able to laugh at it and let go of it. Also remember that you will need to retain enough of a "play = fun" aspect, whether as a Master or slave, or your sex will become work, and sex that is work will soon kill

---

[110] See 27. Slave Identity Drift.

the relationship. This naturally means the two of you should have enough ordinary life interests that you can share together and simply have fun with beyond the Master/slave bond. Before the contract is signed, at least once each week, the potential Master and potential slave should indulge in one such "outside fun" activity, even if it is as simple as going to a mutually interesting movie, and make sure some fun requirement activity is in the contract. This will help to relieve some of the tension that can so easily build up in an M/s relationship. This can also be interpreted as the Master taking the slave out for a weekly reward.

Chapter 42

Novice vs. Experienced Slave

There are advantages and disadvantages for a Master with both a novice (new) slave and an experienced slave. The novice will generally not know what he is really getting into, regardless of how much pre-contract discussion has gone on between the Master and slave. This easily leads to disappointment by one or both parties early on. This is the main reason there should be a short-term (about a month) tryout or pre-contract, in which either party can withdraw without losing face. This might even be followed by a second trial period of about six months. The advantage to a novice slave is that he has no well-established expectations of what a Master should and should not be in contrast to any other Master; thus, the Master may mold the slave as he sees fit.

For a Master acquiring an experienced (formerly owned) slave, the above is reversed. The slave will more or less know what to he is getting into; however, he will have well-established expectations of what the new Master should and should not be. Since each Master is an individual, the new one may resent being compared to the previous Master, much less in some way having the slave try to mold him into that previous Master. Likewise, the experienced slave might resent the new Master trying to remold him into a different kind of slave.

Chapter 43

Maintaining the M/s Relationship

Even once the Master and slave establish that they have been honest enough with each other that it seems like they should start talking about a contract, both have to accept the fact that any M/s relationship is very difficult to maintain over a long period. This is because it depends on both persons being constantly aware of their thoughts, speech, and actions toward one another within their respective status. "Status" here is a key word for the Master/slave relationship, which is not like a simple DS or SM relationship of being on and off the playing stage.[111] Assuming the two live together, as opposed to having separate residences, the Master/slave relationship is an everyday, seven-days-a-week play (drama and comedy), in which the players do not get to leave the stage.

If the Master and slave do live in separate residences part or full time, even when in the slave's residence, the Master behaves as if that residence is his own, and the slave's behavior should be as close as possible to what it is in the Master's residence. If the slave sleeps on the floor in the Master's home, the slave does so in his home; if he does not sleep in the bed in the Master's home without his ritual permission, the slave does not sleep with the Master in the slave's own bed without that permission.[112] Even if the slave is at his home alone he should have received prior permission to sleep

---

[111] For this reason, I have tried to avoid using the word "role," as that implies an on-/offstage relationship.

[112] If the Master is not present, the slave should have asked prior permission from the Master to sleep in his own bed.

in his own bed. Even in the case of the kitchen, the slave does not enter the Master's without the Master's permission. However, the slave does need the right to enter his own kitchen without the Master's prior permission if the Master is not present.[113]

Naturally, an absolute all-day/all-week or 24/7 requiring both parties to live and work together would only exist if both had a job that was performed at home. But this is extremely rare, and one or both parties are more likely to work outside the home and even in separate locations. Any so-called 24/7 would be further reduced if one or both had independent outside activities.[114]

Because any time away from each other is a time to forget one's status, be it Master or slave, it is very important that while the two are together, there is no doubt as to their respective statuses. This basically requires highly ritualized behavior (protocol) by both parties.

(1) Once a contract has been signed, the slave must not call the Master by his legal name without *Master* before it or *Sir* after it. In the non-Scene public, this can be replaced by a pseudonym that acts as a code for Master or Sir.[115] Also, to reinforce their status, the slave should be given a slave name that the Master uses even in public. This need not be anything that will draw unwanted attention, since many people have more than one name. Remember that even vanilla heterosexual couples often have pet names for one another that only they are permitted to use, so there is no reason that anyone should think it strange that the Master/slave in an ordinary public situation might call each other by names other than their birth or legal ones.

(2) Do not act romantically vanilla with each other in public, and even in private, avoid all such designations of each other as *dear, darling, honey, love, sweetheart, baby,* etc. It may be necessary to add the avoidance of such language to the contract, to ensure compliance by both parties.

---

[113] However, while one may not answer the phone in one's Master's house without his permission, the Master may allow the slave this privilege in the slave's own house, because the slave's outside connections may require dealing with it.

[114] Which, in the slave's case, must be approved of by the Master.

[115] See Chapter 6. Use of the Master's Name.

The English word *love* has such a horribly broad meaning, which ranges from the love of parents and spouse to the love of peanut butter. Nonetheless, this does not preclude any Master and slave from saying "I love you." Just don't get "vanilla mushy" about it. If a slave is away from and writing to his Master, "Dear Sir" is acceptable, as it is a common phrase in the business world. Such a letter could then be ended with "Faithfully yours, in fealty," or just "Love, Your slave."

Not only in language but as much as possible in everything else, avoid the seductive power of relaxing into vanilla. This starts with an hour or two a day, then much of a day in a week, then whole days in a month, and soon the M/s status relationship has disintegrated (or evolved, depending on one's view) into more of a scene-specific role activity.

(3) Even if only in private, the slave should be discouraged from using at least first-person pronouns (I, me, my); replacing them with third-person options (the slave's name, this slave, your slave, Sir's toy) or even creating subject-less sentences). [116]

(4) Although it may be problematic while in the general public to enforce the rule that a slave limits his talking when in the presence of his Master, some compromise on this issue might work.[117] However, there should always be some subtle silent signal the Master can give that tells the slave he needs to start just limiting or bring his talking to an end.

(5) To avoid vanilla in public also means that the Master and slave should display a certain degree of emotional distance between them. This is to say that the Master should not show such strong affection for his slave as lightly kissing, holding hands, or giving a cuddly embrace. If the Master/slave kiss in the leather Scene public, it should be one more of lust than of love, the Master forcing his tongue into the slave's mouth. If the slave knows he has the Master's permission, he may reciprocate. The Master may rest his hand and arm on the slave's shoulder or both hands

---

[116] See Chapter 7. Slave Speech.
[117] See Chapter 7. Slave Speech.

on the slave's two shoulders. If for a good reason, the slave may place one hand and arm around the Master's back while having his other arm and hand behind him in slave mode. This stance would be appropriate for picture-taking, assuming it would be inappropriate for the slave to otherwise be on one or both knees in front of or at the side of his Master. This in no way means that intimacy cannot be shown in private, for without such intimacy, neither will feel fulfilled.

In a world where domestic partnership and even same-sex marriage is becoming more and more acceptable, the Master and slave might want to take this route, even though in Western culture, it implies an equality of status between the couple. The fact is that domestic partnership or marriage may be the only way to ensure legal rights and protection for the relationship. If that is the case, when the slave says "I do," he should do so on one (half kneel) or both (full kneel) knees;[118] in the words of the ceremony, the Master should promise to honorably hold and care for the slave, while the slave should promise to honor and obey the Master. This assumes that they can find a person who is in the Scene to marry them; if not, take the next-best alternative. Also, in such a marriage, the old-fashioned words where a wife (slave) promises to obey her husband (Master) might be reintroduced.

(6)   Anytime a slave is to be away from his Master is a good opportunity to reinforce the status. Before departing, even if it is only to go to a daily job, the slave, on his knees, should always formally ask permission from his/her Master to do so. The Master might then take the opportunity to remind the slave that any leaving of the Master is an offense and that the slave may then receive a slap or two on the ass to remind him or her of the slave's violation. Also, when the slave returns to the Master, a similar discipline may be due, with the slave on his knees. This daily discipline really helps keep the roles alive. It should go without saying that the longer

---

[118] See Chapter 11. Kneeling.

the two are apart, the greater the discipline the slave should receive for his or her absence, regardless of the reason for it.[119]

Of course, it could be that it is the Master who, for some reason, must be the one to leave; but even in this case, before his leaving and upon his return, he should immediately reestablish his authority over the slave by whatever means the contract calls for.

(7)   In private, when the slave might need to leave the side of the Master, such as during a meal together, whether he is sitting at the table or on the floor, he should ask permission to do so. Likewise, in public, this permission should be asked, although this may need to be done in some nonverbal manner.[120]

(8)   At home or in a tolerable public social situation, the slave should sit on the floor near his Master's feet.[121] Also, the slave should never sit with his legs or ankles crossed. His legs are always kept spread. The rules of standing, walking, and kneeling should be enforced as much as practically possible.[122]

(9)   If the slave is given the privilege of sleeping in the Master's bed, versus on the floor, an appropriate privileging ritual should precede the slave entering the bed every night. He must never be allowed to think that this is his right, just because he may have been allowed it the previous night.[123]

One of the major ways vanilla creeps into an M/s relationship is through privilege abuse. When a Master gives a slave the right to do something but then either fails to put a time restriction on or ignores the fact that the time has run out, the slave may begin to view the privilege as more of a right. When that happens, it may be hard for the Master to take it away without having to admit he was careless in not monitoring the situation more carefully. Moreover, by that time, the slave may resent it if that is taken away. Thus, as with the bed, if the slave is only allowed in the

---

[119] See Chapter 3. Slave Protocol; Chapter 23. Punishment.
[120] See Chapter 12. Public and Private Eating Behavior.
[121] As slaves get older, getting down and up from the floor may become a problem, in which case a chair is mandated.
[122] See Chapter 10. Standing, Walking, Sitting; Chapter 11. Kneeling.
[123] See Chapter 45. Love and Romance.

kitchen with permission, this permission should be at most for a day, with re-permission given each morning.

(10) The rules for what a slave may and may not clothe himself in and likewise what is exclusive for the Master to wear should be strongly enforced.[124] As soon as the slave returns home, he should be required to remove all his clothing and remain naked or put on something that is never worn outside or in the presence of anyone except his Master. This could include erotic wear. Also, even if a hidden collar was worn during the workday, a special home collar can be put on by the Master.

(11) The rule that the wants of a slave should be subordinate to the wants of his Master could be enforced by the slave requiring permission from his Master to purchase, even with the slave's own money, items the Master might consider unnecessary. This may go as far as the Master confining the slave to a reasonable budget.[125] Since a slave should never outshine his Master, the Master may even require the slave to drive a car of lesser status than that of the Master.

(12) A slave should never challenge a Master's words, actions, or orders in public, even if he is convinced they are wrong. A skillful slave may be able to let his Master know that he (the slave) is having a problem with those words, actions, or orders, by asking for clarification, but unless there is a real threat to health or safety, it is best to follow the Master's lead, rather than ever making the Master seem ridiculous. In private, the slave should have more leeway to question the Master's words, actions, and orders, but any doing so should be within the bounds of what the contract allows.

(13) The Master/slave couple should socialize at least twice a month with one or more other Master/slave couples, or at least with one or more other Masters. In a large city, it is fairly easy to find other such couples or even an entire Master/slave community, especially thanks to the internet. In smaller urban areas, this will be more

---

[124] See Chapters 14–15. Slave Wear I, II.
[125] See Chapter 38. Finances.

difficult, and in rural areas, one may have to go far afield to find others into the Master/slave Scene; but again, the internet may be used to create an entire set of M/s couples to interact with and possibly visit on occasion.

(14) Neither the Master nor the slave should dump a lot of outside stuff on each other. Of course, this is true for even vanilla relationships, but even more so for an M/s relationship. If either party is having a bad time at work or with his family, he should honestly share it with the other, as any close couple should, and yet keep it at enough distance to prevent it from interfering with the relationship.

(15) Make sure that there is a once-a-week time stated in the contract where the Master and slave can leave the authority status to review the ups and downs of the relationship, and regardless of what is said during this time, the slave cannot be punished for it. It is a time that must be regarded as sacred and so above the authority of the material Master.

(16) Both Master and slave should be conscious of the fact that on any day, the level or intensity of the Master's authority may change, in accordance with what the two are involved in on that day. For example, if the Master has decided that the two of them are to go to a sporting event, an amusement park, or the opera, the Master will probably want the slave to think of each other more as equal companions than as M/s. If the slave is ill and the Master is caring for him, the relationship might be more like parent and child, or if the reverse, then the slave may take on the authority of a nurse to the Master as a compliant patient. These are all short-term modifications in authority and should not have any significant impact on the Master's authority otherwise. On the other hand, it would not be inappropriate for the slave, after a day's outing, to get on his knees and thank the Master for the privilege of such equal treatment.

(17) Expect and accept that over time, the relationship will change and the contract will need to be modified (subtracted from and added to). The Master changes the slave, and the slave changes the Master. This means that you grow either more toward each other

or further away from each other. In this, you are no different from a vanilla relationship. To expect that both you and the relationship will not change over time is to set yourselves up for failure.

(18) Some Master/slave relationships might find that, at least for one night or even a twenty-four-hour period each season, a slave might be loaned out to another Master, or two Master/slave couples could trade slaves. This forces the slave out of any complacency he may have fallen into and should rejuvenate his sense of slavehood, while at the same time reminding the Master of his status as an owner of property. Several dungeon parties in a year could also serve this purpose.

(19) A very important issue is that of taking the slave's loyalty and obedience for granted. No one in any relationship wants to be taken for granted, and when that happens, it is guaranteed to sour the relationship. The Master/slave situation is no different in this. In vanilla relationships, periodically bringing flowers and treats home for one's partner or taking him out to dinner works, and it can sometimes work in a Master/slave relationship. However, an M/s relationship has an intensity that requires more than such a vanilla approach. For a slave to be taken for granted can be the equivalent of being ignored, and no one goes into slavery to be ignored. To prevent this or make up for this, the Master must reaffirm the nature of his sub's slavery. One way to let the slave know that his loyalty and obedience are not being taken for granted is for the Master at least once a month to put the slave to a subtle test that the slave will get punished for if he fails. A good slave will generally appreciate this attention to his loyalty. Another way for the Master to let the slave know he is not being taken for granted is to let the slave know that he (the Master) assumes that in the soul of every slave there is lurking a submissive who wants to rebel against his slavery, and that if the Master does not periodically pay special attention to that rebel soul, he will lose his slave. So perhaps once a month, the Master will find some appropriate discipline that *outwardly* tells the slave that he is being punished for that rebel element, but that *inwardly* the

Master values the slave too much to lose him to any potential rebellion. Yes! This is obviously a game that both parties are playing, but that is part of the thrill of an M/s relationship.

(20) The Master and slave should never get lazy about enforcing the contract.[126] This can be a death blow to a Master/slave relationship.

All of the above items can serve to reinforce or intensify the bond between a Master and a slave, but sometimes that very intensity can give rise to a problem. This is Master and/or slave exhaustion or burnout, and if not constructively dealt with, it can lead to a breakup of the relationship.

As might be expected, the burnout problem for a Master is different from that of a slave.

While the slave who needs to relax or even temporarily abandon his status can easily make up for it by going through a resubmission process, which may or may not involve punishment, there is no such easy makeup process for the Master who temporarily needs to relax or abandon his status. In fact, if the Master relaxes his status to any major extent, he may so greatly alienate his slave by this that repair of the relationship may be really difficult. This can be particularly problematic for a Master who has a slave who easily suffers from slave identity drift (SID);[127] and/or for a slave with a dependent personality disorder (DPD). This is a slave who will, sooner or later, start to worry what would happen to him if the Master should tire of him and abandon him. A third slave who can easily cause Master burnout is a slave from hell. This is a slave who is so committed to his status as a slave that he expects his Master to be equally committed to his status as an authority figure. The upshot of this is that this slave may be more committed to the Master image than to the real man, and so any man who could better fit that Master's image would eventually be more attractive to the hell-slave than his current Master. This can leave a Master living in fear of not living up to the standards of his slave, which can only add to any burnout worry.

Clearly, the smart Master should never take on either a DPD slave or hell slave in the first place; any Master who has done so by mistake would

---

[126] See Chapter 51. Contract.
[127] See Chapter 27. Slave Identity Drift.

do well to cut him loose as soon as possible, before the slave turns the Master into a kind of hostage in his own home.

Never forget that it is more difficult to be a Master than to be a slave. The slave submits and obeys, accepts punishment or abandons the relationship. The Master is ultimately responsible for making the decisions that will affect both his life and the life of the slave. Anyone who thinks this is not automatically a great burden to assume has never been a genuine Master.

Caution: Master burnout is not to be confused with "Top drop."[128] This is a state of exhaustion, even depression, a Top may experience after any particularly intense play scene. The exhaustion may be obvious, but the depression can arise from the fact that whereas the submissive may have experienced both intense physical and psychological rewards, the Dom/Master may only experience the psychological reward of dominance. Thus, he may feel that he has done all the work and gotten only half the reward. In any M/s relationship, this drop must be recognized and dealt with by the slave. He needs to counter this drop whenever it happens by verbally or more physically expressing his thanks for his Master's efforts and the gratitude for his Master allowing him to be a slave. Every Master needs this kind of positive feedback if he is to continue to serve the slave's need to be a slave and his own need to be a Master.

While status burnout may be more seriously traumatic for a Master, this is not a reason for downplaying such burnout for a slave. [129] There are any number of reasons for this burnout, including too much control or micromanagement by the Master; spending too much time in high protocol; the failure of the Master and slave to set aside sufficient status-free time to discuss their relationship; the inability or failure of a slave to vent any frustration he has about his relationship in the company of one or more fellow slaves; the Master taking the slave for granted and failing to sufficiently praise him for his service; and the slave having to take on too much responsibility if his Master should get ill or lose his job, etc. In this last case, the slave can go from not being in charge to being in charge

---

[128] See above for "slave drop."

[129] See more on slave drop in Chapter 34. Aftercare.

which, if only for a short time, may not be a problem but if lasting too long can be.

Signs of slave-status burnout may include fatigue, irritability, frustration, hopelessness or despair, a sense of detachment and isolation, a sense of being trapped in the relationship, a developing apathy to the relationship, and finally the loss of trust in the Master and rebelliousness.

Obviously, whatever the cause or causes for this exhaustion, the cure for it will have to start with eliminating the cause or causes; for the slave, this may be as simple as establishing for him a slave space or free space. This is a room or even just a corner of a room where a slave may seek time-out and in which his Master has no authority over him. It is his sanctuary, and he has the right to stay there as long as he needs to. However, if he leaves it for any reason other than to use the toilet or maybe eat, he returns to his Master's authority. If this is just a corner space, it might be separated from the rest of the room by a tall standing screen and should be long enough for the slave to lie down in. This space should be held inviable by the Master and therefore should never be used by the Master to exile the slave to as some punishment or as an alternative to punishment. The slave must choose to enter it of his own free will and never out of threat or coercion.

Another way to deal with slave or Master burnout is a vacation of several days or even a week away from each other. This could be as simple as staying over a few days to a week at the home of a friend or family member. If this is not possible, then at the very least, one or both should leave home early in the morning and not come back until late in the evening (twelve to fourteen hours later). During such off time, they can visit family or friends, go to an amusement park, spend the day at the beach, or in the mountains, etc. Whatever they do should be totally separate or independent of the other person. To symbolize the slave's freedom for this day, he may even be un-collared.

Another way of dealing with status exhaustion (burnout) is that the M/s contract could specify that the private and public lives of the two be kept as separate as practically possible. In other words, the Master/slave relationship is only enforced in private (at home), and although some in the outside world may know of the relationship, they see little or no evidence of it otherwise. However, the home situation could be extended into the semipublic of a leather gathering event.[130]

This private-only approach, however, has its drawbacks, in that the public life of the slave can corrupt him by reminding him of just how free he really is. To counter the corrupting influence of public slave status-dropping, the moment the Master and slave are alone, any equality just before that should be abandoned, and the Master immediately do something to reassert his dominance over the slave. This may go as far as the slave accepting some sort of mild resubmitting, cleansing, non-erotic discipline (symbolic punishment). In fact, such discipline might also be given to the slave just prior to leaving the private sphere to enter the public sphere, as a reminder that he is committing a wrong by leaving the uncorrupted side of his Master for the corrupted side of others. This daily reminder may help keep the relationship alive and fresh. It should go without saying that the longer the two are apart, the greater the discipline the slave should receive for his or her absence, regardless of the reason for it.[131] Of course, it could be that it is the Master who, for some reason, must be the one to leave; but even if this is the case, then upon his return, he should immediately reestablish his authority over the slave by whatever means the contract calls for.

If, despite preventative efforts, burnout occurs, then the only way to ultimately repair the damage may be for the Master and slave to start over again, maybe even with a new contract, one structure to allow for periodic status-dropping. For example, one day a week, perhaps on the Sabbath, the Master and slave may be free to relate to each other as equals. To symbolize this status-dropping, the slave might be temporarily un-collared. This may greatly defuse any future repeat of a burnout situation.

---

[130] This is not the same as keeping the M/s relationship in the closet. Those outside the closet know of the relationship as a private affair.

[131] See Chapter 23. Punishment.

Chapter 44

Manipulating the Master

It is part of every human relationship for some manipulation to occur between partners, but in a Master/slave relationship, a skillful slave learns to carry such manipulation to a high art. After all, this relationship, more than any other kind of relationship, is one of a power exchange, but with the Master technically being the one in charge, it might be difficult to see where a true exchange comes in.[132] Part of the answer to this is that the power of the slave comes from knowing how to get what he wants by subtle manipulation. For example, the slave may manipulate or even seduce the Master with appropriate humbling speech, reminding the Master he is expected to behave in a certain masterly way, that he is to punish or not punish the slave fairly, that he is as much responsible to the slave as the slave is to him, that the contract has as much authority over the Master as it does over the slave.

An experienced Master not only should be aware of this manipulation; he should be surprised if it doesn't happen.[133] The secret to successful slave power is that the slave never pushes his manipulation into the Master's face. In other words, even in those cases where the slave is really in charge of the relationship—not an uncommon situation—the slave never openly challenges the Master's image as being the one in charge, and if such a challenge happens, for whatever reasons, the slave does everything in his

---

[132] See Chapter 45. Love and Romance.
[133] See Chapter 23. Punishment.

power to quickly repair any damage, which may include a manipulated insistence on being punished.

When it comes to the slave manipulating the Master, the worst offenders may be the slave who is a true masochist. This is the slave who gets primary or direct pleasure from the pain inflicted upon him by the Master. If the Master does not satisfy his masochistic needs with sufficiently deserved punishment, he may do things to force the Master to punish him. In this case, the slave may be manipulating the Master to such a degree that one must question who is really in charge; for this reason, an intense masochist rarely makes a good slave. Being less interested in serving a Master than himself, such a masochist would be better getting into a simple sadist/masochist relationship.

Chapter 45

Love and Romance

Love and romance in an M/s relationship have always been controversial. Some Masters believe that love compromises their M/s relationship and try to avoid it altogether. Other Masters believe it is possible to love a slave but not fall in love with the slave—that is to say, not become too attached to or dependent on the slave. Still other Masters do fall in love with their slaves. The slave, naturally, can hold any of these same attitudes, although it is usually more likely for the slave to fall in love with the Master.

The fact is that as time goes by, a Master/slave bond may become so trusting that it is difficult not to see it as anything other than love. The Master would never do anything to break this trust, nor would the slave do anything uncaring toward his Master. I knew of one such loving Master/slave couple who went through an emotional crisis when the older sister of the Master died after a battle with cancer, which devastated the Master, since that sister basically raised him after their mother had died. It literally became the slave's job to help his Master get through the grieving period, which meant that much of the protocol had to be suspended until the Master was able to once again be a Master and not an emotional wreck. The picture of a Master crying in the arms of his slave may seem to reduce his status as an authority figure, but it didn't. A good slave serves his Master in good times and bad, just as a Master takes care of his slave in good times and bad. A slave and Master who are not capable of caring for and comforting one another are not worthy of being called a slave and a Master.

The subject of love, much less romance (romantic love), within an M/s relationship revolves around the issue of punishment. Can a Master be in love with a slave and yet punish him? Remember, as has been mentioned on several occasions, punishment is enough of a component in an M/s relationship that if it is abandoned, even for the sake of love, the M/s relationship falls apart or evolves into something less intense such as a simple Dom/sub relationship.

Love as a problem (detriment) to an M/s relationship tends to be more one for a Master than a slave. For millennia, real (legal) slaves have been known to fall in love with those who punish them, and in the case of voluntary slaves, the punishment is not seen as a sign of unloving, but of loving. In a loving M/s relationship the slave assumes that the Master understands that the slave does not believe that the Master's punishment is aimed at harming the slave, but that that punishment in allowing the slave to go ever deeper into his need to submit. In fact, should the slave begin to sense that a Master no longer believes in himself as a real Master (as opposed to a Dom), it is the slave who will likely feel his status is losing its power and that he is becoming a ghost slave to a ghost Master.

The reason I have heard over and over again for love interfering in an M/s relationship is that as the Master falls in love with the slave, he comes to feel guilty about disciplining, much less punishing the slave. In other words, he experiences the cognitive dissonance of *I love him, yet I must punish him.* The problem with this theory is that the Master, as a reasonable person, knows perfectly well that the slave "loves" the punishment and does not understand why the Master should feel such guilt. In other words, this guilt argument is superficial.

Actually, two separate emotional processes are going on in the Master's head. The first is that when one falls in love, there is a common desire to elevate the object of that love "above" the person in love. This very elevating nature of love is why it is so easy for a slave to fall in love with a Master, since the slave has, from the beginning, elevated the Master above himself. Once a significant amount of trust has been established between the slave and Master, there is little reason the slave would not develop strong love feelings toward the Master.

However, often from the slave's point of view, while he may even want the Master to love him, any such elevation of himself above the Master is likely to be seen as in conflict with, if not a real threat to, the slave's desire (preference) for submission to a Master who alone must naturally be the one elevated above the slave. In other words, to the degree that the Master's love, consciously or subconsciously, is attempting to draw the slave into a far more equal status to the Master, the slave, consciously or subconsciously, may easily interpret that attempt as a betrayal. Of course, in this case, the only real guilt the Master should have is what the slave thinks of as the cruelty of trying to deny the slave his need for total subordination, not equality, in the relationship. The slave's view is clear.

The second emotional process is even more complicated, and it arises from the fact that being a Master with the desire to dominate is generally easier to understand or figure out than being a slave with the desire to submit. Naturally, in a world where dominance is valued over submissiveness, there is little or no mystery as to why someone should wish to dominate another; but why anyone would want to be a submissive is automatically a mystery. This mystery is not only one for those outside the Master/slave world; it is a mystery that no Master, no matter how close to his slave, can or will ever fully understand. In fact, I believe that every honest Master should not only acknowledge this mystery about his slave but also acknowledge that what he doesn't know about his slave should give him a certain sense of fear.

If it can be said that men and women are from different worlds, the same applies between Masters and slaves. This slave mystery, like all mysteries, can both attract and repel, and while it first attracts the Master to the slave, it always has the potential later on to repel the Master from the slave, and this repelling can easily happen as the Master falls in love with the slave. The Master, before falling in love with the slave, wanted only to appreciate the slave's submissiveness, but love can force him to reevaluate his attractiveness to that submissiveness, and the repelling side that was so easily ignored, if not suppressed, can now show itself.

The Master, now in love, does not want to admit that he is repelled by the slave's submissiveness, and guilt over this can become considerable. However, it is not a guilt that can be acknowledged for its true nature, and so it can be relabeled as guilt about being a tyrant over an innocent and helpless slave.

In a sexist world, this guilt is probably far greater in a male/male situation than in a male/female M/s relationship, for the simple reason that a woman, even in a society that supposedly requires gender equality, is still seen as having a certain natural submissiveness; therefore, there is far less reason for her male Master to feel much guilt in loving her while continuing to treat her as his subordinate. How the dynamics of a female/male Master (Mistress)/slave or a female/female Mistress/slave relationship might deal with this love issue I claim no insight into.

Is there any solution to this love issue, or does it automatically mean that most, if not all, M/s relationships in which love shows its disruptive face are ultimately doomed? No, not doomed.

The solution, or at least *a* solution, can be found in a more honest and deeper understanding of the slave by the Master and the Master by the slave. First, the honest Master and honest slave should admit that the two can never really be unequal. Constitutional law sees to this. That law does not allow the slave to ever give up his right to leave his Master, no matter what any contract says or does not say. The slave is a free man, no matter what his fantasy or his Master's fantasy wants to believe. The M/s relationship is a game, a play. The Master, therefore, should recognize that if love requires equality, that equality has been there from the very beginning, so pretending otherwise can only sabotage the future of the relationship.

A second part of the solution is to remember the nature of the slave's empowering humiliation and how that works not to lower his sense of self-worth but to elevate it.[134]

A third part of the solution to the love issue is for the Master to understand as best he can, which is probably not much, that those who are into the deepest level of submission or slavery are mystics. This is to say that they are searching for or have already found an aspect of reality that many of the religious mystics over the millennia have spoken of. Since different slave mystics have different mystical experiences related to their submission, I can only speak of my own—which, by the way, reinforces my non-slave religious experience as a Zen practitioner.

I and other slaves I have communicated with have discovered the uncanny ability to rest contentedly in the present more than any Master can do. There are two reasons for this. First, since the Master technically

---

[134] See Chapter 24. Empowering Humiliation.

has the ultimate authority for all the future planning in the relationship, this leaves him little time to just be in the present. In contrast, the slave, being told he has no such responsibility for himself or the Master, has learned the art of relaxed or calm waiting in the moment, knowing that whatever the Master decides is out of the slave's hands, so he accepts whatever comes.

This is not to be confused with the slave "going under" or entering subspace, that trancelike altered state of consciousness where the slave may actually feel like he has left his body. This can be a wonderful experience for a sub or slave, but also a very precarious one. This is because in this sense of disconnection to his body, the slave may be unable to judge how much pain he can safely take, and he may even be unable to communicate with his Master. Even momentarily forgetting how to breathe has also been reported in such subspace.

The second reason for the slave to be in the present is that the fully committed slave has developed the wisdom to know the difference between needs and wants. He needs very few things to live (food, water, a modest place to dwell, a minimum amount of clothes, and whatever medicine a health issue may require). All of these can be obtained by the average slave either on his own or through his Master. Everything beyond these survival needs are wants, and wants are endless, except in an M/s authentic relationship. This is because wants are only what his Master agrees to, which means that only the more inexperienced slave is attached to his wants. The slave may want to go to a movie, but the Master says no. The wise slave does not resent this but says to himself, *The Master has spoken. I have been reminded that I am a slave. No movie could be more important than that "no." I am at peace with myself and it.* On the other hand, if the Master says yes, the slave says to himself, *My Master has given me a gift. It is not anything I earned, for I am a slave. I am at peace with myself and it.*

It may be difficult for non-M/s people to understand, but for some slaves, their being owned is a religious experience.

The Master who can appreciate something like this mystical contentment of his slave, rather than being repelled by the slave's submissiveness, might better feel envy for something the Master's will never let him experience. Perhaps such envy can be put to the good use of keeping the Master attracted to that slave's submissiveness and by doing so, in some way experience vicariously that contentment and to love the slave for it.

There is one other way that, despite love, non-erotic discipline (punishment) can be kept alive in an M/s relationship. This is to give the contract, not the Master, the responsibility to decide when and how the slave is to be punished. For example, if the contract says that the slave must be flogged once a week, the Master must not do otherwise. If the contract says that the slave must be spanked, belted, caned, or paddled each night before he has the right to sleep in the Master's bed, the Master must do it, regardless of his personal feelings on the issue.[135] This is another reason a contract is so important.

Also, it should be remembered that most of the time when the Master and slave are at home, they are at level-one protocol, which allows for a level of equality that should be easily open to love and affection. Also, after any kind of sex, whether heavy or light, the Master and slave have an opportunity to reduce inequality to a minimum as long as being a Master and slave remains primary and being lovers-spouses remains secondary.[136]

---

[135] In most cases, just getting on one's knees and thanking the Master for such bed privileges is enough.

[136] Naturally, when a Master and slave love each other, it should be as two mutually identified adults, not as a parent and child. That love should be reserved for the Daddy/boy relationship.

Chapter 46

Disabled Masters/Disabled Slaves

I have encountered several individuals who would, under the right circumstances, make either a good Master or a good slave, but they are prevented from this because of prejudice about physical disability. The disability may make the disabled person feel unqualified or feel regarded by others as unqualified. The first thing that everyone in the Master/slave community should remember is that being a Master or being a slave is as much a state of mind as it is of body. I knew of a man who had been a flogging Master but was in an accident that left him in a wheelchair. He became convinced that his days of flogging were over because no one would want to be flogged by a cripple. What he needed to be reminded of was that there are far more men out there who want to be flogged than who want to flog, and once he was convinced of this, he found a number of men who were willing to bottom for him in this activity, and one of those became a full-time sub. Also, I knew a potential slave who, in the military, had lost a hand and had a steel prosthetic replacement. He thought that since he would never attract a Dominant, he might as well not even try. Once convinced to go to leather meetings and even become a volunteer for their activities, he ended up with a leather husband/Master. In two other M/s pairs, one partner was blind. In the first pair, it was the Master, and to deal with this, his slave always wore a small bell on his chain collar, so that the Master could always hear where he was. In the second pair, it was the slave who was blind. Many people wondered how a blind slave could serve a Master, but since that slave was a sex slave, not a domestic one, there was no problem. No one needs sight to have sex.

Chapter 47

Transgendered Master/Slave Relationship

I have only a limited experience with such relationships. I knew of a female-to-male slave with a male Master, and I have heard of a transgendered male-to-female slave with a male Master, and a similar transgendered slave to a Mistress. I have even heard of a transgendered (female-to-male) Master with a non-transgendered slave. While I have not yet heard of any M/s relationships in which both parties are transgendered, I know no reason why they should not exist.

More common is a Master or slave who is a cross dresser (transvestite), and I did know one M/s situation where both the Master and slave were into gender-bender fucking. This is where one gender may wear the clothes of the opposite gender but without any attempts to disguise the wearer's real gender. In the case I knew the best, the Master and the slave both would dress in female clothes, but since they both had heavy beards, there was no attempt to really appear as women.

Chapter 48

Alpha Submissive/Slave

There are two kinds of alpha slaves: the senior kind and the training kind. In the first, the alpha slave is simply a senior slave in a household with two or more slaves. The senior designates the slave who has been with the Master the longest. This slave is to be respected, if nothing else, for his or her seniority, which means he or she may get some perks the other(s) may not. The training alpha slave more often than not is also the senior one; however, helping a Master train one or more other (newbie or wannabe) slaves requires a certain personality and skill that simple seniority does not always imply. In this case, a full trained slave (beta) with less seniority might be chosen for the training alpha position, provided that that training alpha still recognizes that he or she is still expected to show deference to the senior alpha.

When it comes to slave training, all slaves are classified as gammas, betas, or alphas.

The gamma is a slave who is in training. The beta is one who has finished training and can either remain with the training Master or go on to find a new Master. The alpha is a fully trained beta slave his Master uses as an assistant trainer, and who can even petition his Master to have his own personal gamma or slave. However, it should be made clear that a training alpha, even with his own gamma, is not a Master and will continue to crave to be himself under a Master.

The problem with being an alpha is that it is easy to become overbearing, and when this happens, the alpha either accepts some really humiliating form of punishment or is demoted to a beta, either temporarily or permanently. I knew of one alpha who made this mistake once and paid for it. The Master offered the alpha a choice of three punishments: (1) He may not communicate verbally with the Master or other slaves for up to two weeks but must communicate entirely in written form on pages of a small pad of paper which, once shown, must be chewed up and swallowed; or (2) after being man-milked[137] he must submit to a number of lashes given by the Master or the gamma(s) he had wronged, but with the number of lashes determined by the Master. These lashings could be of any intensity the flogger chooses. (3) The alpha must, for one week, wear a locked cock cage that prevents him from having a full erection, much less masturbating; this sometimes includes him standing in slave mode while witnessing any sexual relations the Master might be having with another slave. The cage does not prevent the Master from fucking the alpha.

The alpha chose the second punishment for several reasons. The first punishment technically was something even a vanilla person could deal with, and the alpha was not vanilla. Also, it stretched the punishment out too long for the alpha's taste. The third meant that unless the Master fucked the alpha or allowed him to suck the Master off, the alpha might have no physical contact with the Master for that week, and no real slave wants that. It is like being a dog that desperately wants you to pet him and you refuse.

The second punishment, although the painful one, had the advantage of being done and over within an hour or less; besides, the alpha had never experienced that kind of punishment, and, being an inquisitive masochist, he decided it was time to experience such punishment. Also, the alpha was very sure it was this punishment that his Master hoped he would choose, and to make up for disappointing the Master, the slave figured this would do it.

After the Master had another slave suck the alpha dry, the Master turned the alpha over to the gamma who had been over punished, to be flogged with a vengeance. However, once the Master had decided that the slave had had enough, the gamma made the serious mistake of saying to

---

[137] Being forced to ejaculate so that he is no longer sexually aroused by the punishment.

the Master, "Let me give him one more." To this the gamma received, in the enraged words of the Master, "When I say enough, I mean enough. This was a serious punishment, not a game to entertain you."

The alpha was immediately removed from the flogging cross, got down on his knees, and said, "Thank you, Master, for your kindness in making me realize what a poor slave I am. The punishment is far less than I deserve. I have shown myself unworthy to receive your trust, and whatever further punishment I am to receive, I humbly accept it."

The offending gamma was then put on the cross and flogged by the Master for his impertinence. To this alpha's surprise, his alpha status was reinstated after only one week without further punishment.

Technically one's alpha status is suspended once the slave leaves the service of the Master who recognized it and remains suspended until one is under a new Master, who will hopefully re-recognize it. However, it is not unheard of that after leaving a Master's service and before finding a new Master, an alpha may cheat with this suspended status and continue to refer to himself as a training alpha slave when either (a) another sub (more correctly a naïve one) approaches him or (b) the alpha is trying to determine if a man he is interested in is not an obvious Dom or sub. In either case, he may say, "I'm an alpha slave, which means that as a slave I'm a submissive, but as an alpha I can also dominate, so it would be helpful to know which you might prefer, that is assuming you are interested in either of those."

Chapter 49

Master/Slave Families

This generally refers to a Master with two or more slaves, although there are M/s families of two or more Masters/Mistresses with one or more slaves (all male, all female, or mixed). Personally, I have experienced only a male Master and me, a male Master plus me plus a toy-boy, and two male Masters and me. I have no insight regarding how families run by Mistresses work, nor those with mixed-gender slaves. Families with one or more Masters tend to be unstable due to conflicts with who has authority priority, although I have heard about one such family that has been going well for several years. In another case, the two Masters and the one slave each live separately, with the slave rotating between the Masters.[138]

The obvious problem for a Master with multiple subs is that as the authority figure, he alone has to balance the different needs and wants of those subs, to avoid conflict and rebellion.

In a household with two or more slaves, there is always the problem that the Master will favor one slave more than another. This is always a bad situation in that it will (not *may*) lead to conflicts that may cause the Master to lose one or both slaves. The skillful Master will be ever aware of this and take measures to make sure that regardless of his feelings, he makes all his slaves feel equally valued and wanted.

To feel equally valued and wanted, however, does not mean that all

---

[138] One Master on M/T/W and the other on Th/F/Sa with Sunday the day all three get together, or the Masters alternated, or the slave had off.

slaves need to be treated equally. An alpha (senior) slave must be given more privileges than a non-senior slave, and those non-seniors who do not understand and accept this protocol should be dumped by the Master, because they are nothing but trouble. A Master may have two or more slaves who serve different functions, in which case they may be treated differently but in an equal way. For example, one slave may be mainly a sexual one, while another is mainly a domestic one, but anything that might look like favoritism need not be if spelled out in the contract. Even where both slaves might be sexual ones, each may function differently sexually. For example, one slave may be able to tolerate and even desire flogging, while another cannot.

In another situation, a Master had a main slave and an auxiliary slave. The first lived with the Master, while the second did not and was with the Master and main slave only midweek and weekends. The main slave, knowing he had the Master to himself most of the week, did not mind the extra attention the auxiliary slave received for those few days.

Naturally, potential favoritism can work in reverse. For example, if two Masters share a slave and that slave favors one Master over the other, this situation they will soon end their relationship if the two Masters cannot fix it.

Chapter 50

Guardian Master

Sometimes a Master may need to be away from the slave for a week or more, and he does not wish for the slave to feel suddenly free, much less abandoned, and so he may find another Master to act as a guardian authority for the slave. That guardian must be acceptable to both the Master and slave, and it must be understood that the guardian is under the same contract conditions as the Master and slave. This fact should be clearly stated and even put in writing.

A temporary ownership ritual will usually be performed, which may or may not involve a pissing baptism. In most cases, the sense of authority of the real Master will be retained, if possible, by a daily phone call or email from the Master to the slave. During these communications, the slave would be expected to use a code to tell the Master whether or not he was being properly treated. If the slave opened the communication with the very formal greeting, "Hello, Master X," this meant that the guardian was treating the slave well. If it opened with the less formal "Hello, Sir," it meant the slave was not happy but he could tolerate the situation. If the opening was an informal "Hello," it told the Master that the slave wanted him to tell the guardian to release him on his own, for there were problems. If the slave greeted the Master with what amounts to near rudeness, "Hi," it meant the slave was in an emergency and that the Master needed to contact the silent alarm partner[139] the Master had previously arranged for, or if that person could not be reached, then the police should be called.

---

[139] See Chapter 31. Silent Alarm Partner.

Chapter 51

The Contract

Although it is probably obvious to most readers that an M/s contract has no real legality to it, that is to say, it would not be honored in a court of law, nonetheless, this fact should be clearly acknowledged by the signers. This naturally leads to the question why have such a contract? In the M/s relationship, the contract serves several very important functions.

(1) A contract encourages the Master and slave to communicate to each other exactly what they expect and do not expect out of the relationship.

(2) A contract is a record of what those expectations are and are not. Masters and slaves may forget some specifics of what was originally negotiated, and the contract is there to remind them. Without this reminder, it seems that a Master or a slave can easily misremember, especially as the weeks and months go by.

(3) A contract makes it very clear to both signers that their relationship is not that of a Daddy/boy, a simple Dom/sub, or a scene-specific activity. What is being signed up for is something of far greater commitment and intensity.

(4) A contract may be especially important to a person who is entering slavery for the first time, as that is a very scary adventure. The clear limitations worked out by both parties should help to alleviate a considerable amount of that scariness.

(5)   By the fact that the contract is a higher authority than the Master, it can help to sustain the M/s relationship if the Master, falling in love with the slave, begins to question his right of dominance.[140]

(6)   No matter how many Doms or Masters I had unofficially submitted to, it was not until I actually lived as a slave under a contract that I could be certain that my sense of being a slave was more than something superficial, which I could easily take hold of and let go of. In other words, being under a contract made me realize for the first time that being a slave did not depend on whether or not I had a Master; I simply was a slave.

No contract is going to be perfect, and over time, it will have to be modified in accordance with the inevitable changes in the lives of its signers. Whatever these may be, it must be understood by both Master and slave that the ultimate authority in an M/s relationship is not the Master but the contract. The contract is not only the constitution for the relationship but the sacred text for it. As such, it is the violation of it by either party that should constitute the most punishable offense. This offense, unlike other offenses, must be squarely laid on the offender, which means the slave cannot be punished for the Master's violation of the contract, and if he is the guilty party, he alone must find a way to atone.

For those who bad-mouth contracts as something that interferes with the right of a Master to demand unconditional obedience from a slave, I would remind them that there are a lot of unstable people out there, and the kinky world seems to attract more of them than the vanilla world. While negotiating a contract will not ferret out all of these, such negotiations will help discover who many of them are, if for no other reason than the insincere Master or slave has little patience for anything but the most minimal negotiations. Also, most such unstable Masters or slaves will have difficulty in finding reliable witnesses to sign a contract.

Another major complaint I have heard about negotiating a contract is that it is either really boring or takes the thrill out of finding a Master or a slave. A related complaint is that negotiating is so coolly technical that it robs finding a Master of any romance. For such complainers, I say, "If you

---

[140] See 45. Love and Romance.

are going to turn over much of your life to another, you had better know what that other wants and does not want, or you will regret it."

Sample Slave Contract

The sample contract below has been compiled from three different, much shorter actual contracts between Masters and slaves. Therefore, it is not to be assumed that all M/s contracts should follow exactly this format. Each M/s relationship is unique, and so the contract that goes with it must be. Nonetheless, this author feels that this sample offers enough of a pattern upon which more individual contracts could be based. In other words, items could be deleted and/or added to suit the special requirements of the signers. Also, this contract represents what a fully trained slave might commit to and should not be thought of as something to even show a slave in training (a gamma), as it might scare him off. It is therefore advised that something far less committal might be offered him or her until he or she is ready for the big plunge.

Some Masters actually offer two or more levels of contracts. There may be a getting-to-know-each-other contract of a month or so. There are very few obligations in this one, and either party can dissolve it unilaterally, simply because their relationship does not feel right. Then there is a training contract, which will have more obligations, will have an ending date of three months to a year, and will have serious reasons for ending the contract before its date. This contract can be extendable for a few months at a time. Finally, there is a full contract with no less than a yearlong limit or no specific stated one; however, some clause should be added that allows for periodic changes/updates.

It is the feeling of this contracted slave of many years that extra attention should be given to the final section of any contract: "The conditions under which either the Master or slave could rightly terminate the contract." Extra attention here hopefully serves to make both Master and slave aware that any dissolving of the contract is not only an issue between each of them but may affect their standing in the larger M/s community. This will be true even if that larger community consists only of the preferred four witnesses to the original signing.

To start with, any negotiations between a Master and slave should be done while the slave is still free and more or less on an equal footing with the Master. Any conflicting views during that time cannot be judged as a challenge to the Master's authority; but once the contracted play begins, any attempt to negotiate may be seen as such a challenge.[141] Also, a first-time contract with a Master that the slave still does not know well should be for only one or three months, which is usually sufficient time to figure out whether or not the slave wants to commit to a longer contract, say six months, and then to a still longer one. No first-time contract should be for a 24/7 period. Both the Master and slave still need time away from each other to evaluate the relationship.

(I) The first section gives the definitions of what Master and slave have agreed upon as to what a slave is, as far as this contract is concerned. These definitions should be part of the very first negotiations and continue until both come up with what is compatible enough to suggest that they can work/play together. Any Master/slave pair who does not deal with this definition issue soon is setting themselves up for failure.

(a) The slave is a submissive who has agreed to all the items in this contract and nothing outside it unless further agreed upon and amended by both the Master and this slave.

(b) The slave has only one Master, that being the one who has signed this contract.

(c) The slave at all times will show deference to the Master, with the full understanding that not to do so will result in punishment in accordance with the punishment section below.

(d) The slave will at first be subject to total domination by the Master and must earn the right of gradual leniency.

(e) The slave, for the purposes of this contract, is basically a sex slave (domestic slave, show slave, pet slave), and has no regular

---

141 This makes for another distinction between a simple submissive and a slave. The former can renegotiate a situation with his Dominant at any time, even after being collared, while a slave gives this right up once collared. Property does not get negotiated.

domestic duties, although such a duty might be part of some punishment.[142]

(II) The second section deals with the contractual times of service. For example, is the slave a 24/7 slave or less? For example, if the two do not live together, it might read,[143]

(a) Excluding the slave's outside employment hours, he will serve the Master the evenings of Tuesday, Thursday, Saturday, and following mornings, which means before any necessary outside employment; also, he will serve all day Sunday, and Monday morning.

(b) Monday, Wednesday, and Friday evenings and their following mornings will be the slave's to do as he wishes except to trick out.[144]

(c) This is not a Full Disclosure Contract; therefore, the slave is not "required" to report every activity he does on his free time, nor does he have to disclose anything supposedly said to him in private or confidence unless it directly affected the M/s relationship.[145]

---

[142] This was in all my contracts; thus, this slave was not responsible for cleaning the Master's home, although I did volunteer outside the contract to cook some breakfasts and dinners. The only domestic punishment that would be assigned to me was that of cleaning the Master's bathroom floor on my hands and knees. However, if the slave is only or partly a domestic, the contract should say so.

[143] Actually, even for what is expected to become a 24/7 relationship, it is best that the Master and slave continue to have separate residences for the first few months or even up to a year. This transition period will, in most cases, help to ensure that any later 24/7 will go more smoothly.

[144] Since no first-time slave can be sure how much service time he can deal with, something like this is advisable.

[145] Some Masters insist on such a full disclosure as a way of ensuring exclusive loyalty of the slave to the Master. Keeping information from a Master that does not involve him is very different from being secretive, much less lying, which is more of a sin than any disobedience. A slave who lies should be open to immediate dismissal unless there are real extenuating circumstances. Did the slave lie to protect someone else? Did he lie because he was ashamed of something he did and was afraid his Master would think him unworthy and dump him? These could be forgivable sins. Or did he lie to avoid punishment? This is not forgivable.

(d)   This schedule will cover a full twenty-six (26) weeks or six (6) months, at which point the Master and slave will reevaluate the contract. Subtracting the days of the week the slave has off (3 x 26 or 78) means that he will be in service for 104 days total. Also, whenever below a full weekly period is mentioned, that implies Saturday night to Saturday night.

(III) The third section of the contract outlines the slave's responsibilities and the

Master's responsibilities.

(a)   The slave will never greet the Master with a common "Hello" or "Hi," but with a full "Good morning (afternoon, evening, or night), Sir! If in public, and the honorific "Sir!" might be too attention-getting, the slave may substitute his hand placed over his heart for the "Sir," but only on such an occasion.[146]

(b)   On those agreed-upon days of service that the slave is not with the Master all day, such as on the slave's outside work days, he will call or text a midday message to the Master stating where he is at that time.

(c)   If the slave, during agreed-upon service days, is to be absent for more than ten (10) hours of outside work, the slave must check in with the Master by phone or email every five (5) hours, detailing his location and reason for being there, unless this was authorized by the Master in advance. Any violation of this rule will lead to punishment. If returning to the Master after an absence of more than twelve (12) but less than twenty-four (24) hours, the slave will undergo the minimum service-renewal discipline. In this, the slave will assume the crouching position on the floor in front of the Master with the slave's butt bare, so as to receive the reconnecting power of the Master's hand and/

---

[146] See Chapter 6. Use of the Master's Name/Title.

or belt.[147] If the slave is out of service for more than twenty-four (24) hours, the slave may be required to undergo a more extensive service-renewal discipline (minor punishment). This may entail the renewed ownership (pissing-on) baptism. In the case of a slave who will be out of such service three times a week, he may be required to undergo the major punishment three times a week. All this will be at the Master's discretion.

(d) Except for passing through security devices, etc., the slave will keep his chain (dog) collar or an alternative on unless removed by the Master.[148] Even on those three (3) times a week the slave has off, if possible, he should keep his collar on his person (in a pocket) at all times.[149] This collar may have a dog tag that says, "Property of Master X" and the beginning and ending dates the slave is under contract.

(e) Without the Master's specific order, the slave will never kneel before another Master. Instead, he will assume the appropriate stance, and if needing to verbalize a greeting will say, "Sir! In the name of my Master, this slave is honored to meet you. Sir!"[150]

(f) When with the Master, the slave will be available for some level of sex at any time, unless the slave has a very legitimate reason,

---

[147] An M/s relationship is not a D/s relationship in which the Dom has limited authority over the sub. The Master's total authority over the slave means that anytime the slave is away from (not under) the Master's authority is an offense, and the slave who does not expect to pay for this offense would do better to be in a D/s relationship.

[148] The slave could be required to wear a special bracelet or ankle chain instead. A cock-and-ball ring would be even better.

[149] Some Masters want the slave to wear their leather color under a shirt and tie, but be aware that a leather collar that is not naturally black (that has been dyed) can bleed that color if exposed to a lot of neck sweat, so if one is wearing it under a shirt with a tie, it might bleed onto the shirt collar. This could be embarrassing. This is why a chain collar is better under a shirt and tie.

[150] It is not uncommon for a slave, upon introduction to another Master, to be ordered to assume a kneeling position; but some Masters are not willing to let their slaves show that much deference to another Master. However, if the other Master is a former one of the slave, some special deference should be shown him unless the relationship ended very badly.

such as illness.[151] Otherwise, if he says no, he understands that he will be punished within no more than twelve (12) hours of the offense. Before being given the privilege of being fucked by the Master, the slave will present his butt to the Master's hand, belt, cane, paddle, or flogger. This will be the slave's diplomatic sign of fealty to the Master. Such diplomacy before sodomy can be summarized as "No pleasure before pain." The slave may be required to perform anal service while standing, lying on his stomach, side, or back, or on all fours at any time of the day or night that his Master wishes.[152]

(g) Whenever the slave receives the Master's member for either oral or anal intercourse, the Master will wear a condom, and any oral-anal sex will require a clean and healthy anus.[153] To help ensure that the slave is always fresh for the Master's appreciation, the slave will wash his asshole off with soap and/or alcohol after every use of the toilet. For this reason, the slave, if not at home, is required to keep a supply of alcohol prep pads in his pocket along with a condom and package of lube in case the Master wants to rim or even fuck him in a private lockable restroom.

(h) The Master may have another occasional play partner without the slave's objections, but the slave, as personal property, may have another partner only with the Master's permission.[154]

---

[151] This applies to a sex slave, not necessarily to a domestic.

[152] The "at any time" requirement creates an element of surprise lacking in most other relationships. In those others, straight or gay sex is usually compartmentalized into a bedtime activity, but the Master demanding sex outside of that time and demanding such unexpected sex two or three times a week serves to reinforce his position as the one sexually and otherwise in charge. The reason for the position details is because in some contracts, the one position some Masters will not fuck his slave in is the deep stick. In this position, the bottom lies on his back with legs raised over the Top's shoulders, who can then fuck from a kneeling position. In this position, the Master and slave would be viewing each other's faces, and a few Masters feel this is too personal. On the other hand, other Masters get off on watching the expression on the slave's face as the Master plows into him.

[153] This requirement means that the slave need not rim any Master with anal warts.

[154] This assumes the slave is not in a slave family.

(i) The Master will do his best to satisfy the slave's sexual fantasies at least three times a week, and more if the Master chooses.[155]

(j) During warm weather, the slave, while at the Master's home and except during sleep, will wear his slave harness, a butt plug, a jock strap, and other desired erotic wear (ex. socks and boots). While dressed like this, the slave will not normally answer the doorbell, but will retreat into another room until the Master tells him otherwise. During cold weather, the slave may wear around the Master's home a long-sleeved shirt and long pants, but the latter must not be buttoned or belted as to prevent immediate access to the slave's cock or ass. Therefore, only pants that can be instantly pulled down will be permitted.

(k) For the first week or two, the slave will sleep with a pillow and sheet and/or blanket on a futon or air mattress on the floor next to the Master's bed.[156] Once the slave has earned the further right, he may sleep in the Master's bed, but only after paying for this right each night with a mild spanking, belting, caning, or paddling, unless he has been sufficiently flogged earlier that evening. The Master may withdraw the right of the slave to sleep in his bed at any time or for any reason. Twice a week, in lieu of spanking, etc., the Master can require the slave to give the Master a full-body and feet massage. Whether in the bed or on the floor, the slave will always sleep naked from at least the waist down. Anytime the slave is sleeping on the floor, it will be with his Master's boots next to him.

Obviously, this means that the slave will not retire before the Master has, to ensure any of the Master's needs are taken care of beforehand. Moreover, before the Master falls asleep, the slave, in a standing position with arms behind his back, should state,

---

[155] Every contract should contain specific details about the fantasies versus realities of the Master and slave. For any Master/slave pair who have not first come to a clear and mutual understanding of this distinction, the relationship at the very start is in trouble.

[156] Remember that the normal place for a slave to sleep is on the floor. It is best to start out with the slave accepting this situation and assign at least one night a week for the slave to do so.

"Master X, thank you for permitting me to be your slave. This is an honor and privilege, and I hope I have lived up to it today."

(l)   To keep his slavery fresh, the slave should consider each morning as if it were the first one in the life as a slave, and so a symbolic initiation should be undergone. Before the Master gets out of bed, the slave, on his knees, will greet the Master with "Good morning, Sir! How may I serve you today?"[157] Obviously, for this to happen, the slave should never oversleep, and if he does, it is a punishable offense.

While for in some M/s relationships, this may mean that the slave will arise before the Master and be dressed appropriately, this is not desired by those Masters who feel that the slave should still be in bed should the Master wakes up and wants immediate sexual gratification.[158]

(m)   When, after a period of an hour or more of absence, the Master enters a room that the slave is in, the slave will immediately stand with his arms behind his back unless holding something he cannot conveniently lay down. The slave will not leave the room his Master is in without either asking for permission to do so and/ or explaining why he is leaving his Master's presence.

(n)   The slave has no privacy from the Master; therefore, he will never close a door to a room he is in that might separate him from the Master without specific permission. The Master, however, may close a door for privacy. This will include the bathroom. In fact, when the slave is in the bathroom, the Master may enter at any time unannounced, but if the Master is in the bathroom, the slave may enter only with permission.

(o)   When the Master and slave are walking down a street, the slave will always walk on the Master's dominant-hand side. If the there is a second sub, the senior one will be on the non-dominant side and the junior one on the dominant side.

---

[157] One Master I had responded by pushing the slave's head to the ground and placing his foot on the back of the slave's neck while giving him his first order of the day.

[158] This was the case with one of this author's Masters, who often did not even wait until this slave woke up before the Master was ready to fuck him.

(p)   When the Master and slave need to go out in the Master's car, if the Master is driving (the usual situation), the slave will wait to open the passenger door until the Master has opened his door; moreover, the slave will not sit down until the Master has done so. If for any reason the slave must drive the Master somewhere, the same rules will apply. It is not necessary for the slave to open the car door for the Master unless there is some unusual reason to do so. The slave will exit the car before the Master, so as not to still be sitting while the Master is standing.

(q)   When at home, the slave may, with permission, sit on the couch when alone with the Master, but when the Master has company, the slave will sit only on a cushion on the floor near the Master's feet unless told otherwise. However, the slave must not sit before the Master does, and when the Master stands, so must the slave, unless allowed otherwise.[159] However, for dining purposes, the slave, while permitted to eat his meals at the table with the Master, may be required to sit on a backless slave seat (tall stool).

(r)   In public, such as in a restaurant, the slave will wait for the Master to sit and will stand at the same time as the Master. The one exception is if either the Master or slave needs to use the restroom, a need the slave will ask permission for. Also, the slave will ask permission from the Master as to what the slave is permitted to eat. The slave may not start eating until the Master begins, nor continue to eat once the Master has finished.

(s)   When it comes to the issue of food, the Master will respect any special dietary habits of the slave, and unless the Master is paying for a meal, the slave may choose his own food, but not if it is more expensive than that of the Master. Also, the slave will be aware of what the Master might find offense food-wise and not eat it in front of him.

(t)   The slave will keep all the Master's sex toys clean, even if they had been used on another bottom; and above all else, the slave will make sure the Master's boots are clean and polished at all

---

[159]   As noted in Chapter 10. Standing, Sitting, and Walking, if the slave in sitting on the floor, he may not need to stand each time the Master does.

times. Any dereliction of duty in this regard will result in instant punishment.

(u)   To remind the slave of his slave position, once each week he may be required to submit to a light to moderate non-erotic (outside of any sexual scene) discipline. This will be a hand, belt, cane, or flogger on the slave's butt. *Light to moderate* means not as intense as such discipline is given during sex. As to ensure that this is clearly not erotic in any way, the slave will have to be de-aroused (forced to cum, milked) beforehand, so it may be best to undergo this reminder soon after a regular sex scene. Neither this nor any other physical punishment will be carried out beyond the slave calling out the safe word, which is "wimp, wimp, wimp."

At the end of such reminder-punishment, the slave will say, "Thank you, Master, for your kindness of reminding this slave of his obligation as a loyal and faithful submissive."

(v)   If the slave, for whatever reason, feels he needs to or is about to express anger toward the Master, the slave will immediately assume a kneeling position in front of the Master and wait until the Master is ready to hear the reason. The Master himself will not leave his position until the slave has had at least five minutes to express himself. This kneeling position of the slave before his Master may also be used if the slave feels he needs the Master's full attention on some matter of importance to either the slave or Master. In public, this kneeling position will be replaced by the slave holding his right fist over his heart to get the attention of the Master.

(w)   If the slave is unsure if a particular action might displease the Master, it is the slave's responsibility to ask the Master. If not asked, the Master may punish the slave for the action. Even if the slave feels that the Master should have previously warned him about the offensiveness of the action, that is not an acceptable excuse. So, the slave should not make matters worse by expressing that feeling. He should simply learn from his punishment. Be aware that the Master who never entices a slave into a punishable action is a Master that a slave will never take seriously.

(x)   The Master and slave will not use any romantically familiar designations toward one another that might imply a real level of equality such as *dear, darling, honey*,[160] *love, sweetheart, baby,* etc. However, in a formal email, the slave may open with "Dear Sir" and close with "Faithfully Yours, Xxxx." If the Master should mistakenly use such an endearment, it is the slave's responsibility make the Master aware of that situation. If he does not, that is a punishable action.

(y)   A period of two hours a week will be set aside for Master and slave to leave their inequality just enough to communicate with one another freely about how the relationship is working or not working without any threat of reprisals.

(z)   The Master will never require the slave to do anything the slave feels is illegal.[161]

(IV) Extra-sexual activities.

(a)   The slave will not masturbate without the Master's permission, as this may make him less interested in serving the Master at any time.

(b)   The Master, as a gratuity, on occasion has the right to loan his slave property out to another Top for play purposes, but only under the Master's supervision, to ensure no maltreatment of his property or that the contract has been violated.

(c)   Playing with another Top will be confined to simple vanilla fellating or anal intercourse, but not any SM activities or oral-anal sex unless agreed upon by both the Master and the slave.

(d)   If it is the pleasure of the Master, this slave may be requested to top another bottom.

(e)   Unless it is for punishment for a really serious infraction on the part of the slave, he will not be loaned out to anyone the slave considers completely unacceptable. In fact, even for punishment

---

[160] Honey: To be said only in reference to what a Master may pour on his dick to make a slave thoroughly lick it off.

[161] Obviously, in the past, when sodomy laws were still enforced, the Master and slave were both doing something illegal.

purposes, the proposed loaner will be deemed unacceptable if the slave feels his health or safety may be compromised. Also, any such punishment cannot be used more than once in this contract period.

(**V**) Section five deals with activities that would be unacceptable to the slave.

(a) No burning (fire play) or mutilation. Hot wax permitted if not too intense.[162]

(b) Nothing that would result in broken bones or torn skin.

(c) Nothing that involves drawing or releasing of blood.

(d) Nothing that might impede breathing or circulation. Therefore, due to the slave's asthmatic condition, only gags that do not do so;[163] thus, holding the slave's soiled jockstrap or butt plug[164] in his mouth is acceptable. Also, as a punishment in and of itself, the slave could tolerate carrying between his teeth for up to two hours the cane or belt usually used on him for non-erotic pain (punishment).[165]

(e) No electric shock including no violet wand.[166]

(f) Nothing resulting in a loss of consciousness or damaging of any of the senses.

---

[162] Hot wax: Relatively safe way to use heat for erotic pleasure, but the clean-up is torturous.

[163] Gag: A reminder to the sub or slave that speech is a freedom he has no right to.

[164] This doesn't sound particularly sanitary, much less healthy, but remember that one is essentially immune to any of one's own anal material that might be on the plug.

[165] There is a very good reason for not allowing an unfamiliar Top to gag a sub. The gagged sub cannot scream out for help if the scene is wrong. See information in Chapter 31. Silent Alarm Partner (SAP).

[166] Violet wands were originally electric and neon testers used for the application of low-current, high-voltage (min 35 kV to max 65 kV typically), high-frequency electricity to the body; as such, they are most commonly used in BDSM though erotic-sensation play. Violet wands can deliver a variety of sharp, cutting, or piercing sensations.

(g) No administering of alcohol or drugs.[167] The Master will not be under the influence of these during sex.

(h) No extremes of temperature.

(i) No scat (shit) of the Master's or the slave's on any part of the slave or Master's body. This is a hard limit.

(j) No foreign urine in the slave's mouth.[168] Also, the slave will not be subjected to more than his Master's piss without the slave's permission; more specifically no group pissing scene.

(k) No sleep deprivation. If the Master in the middle of the night should awaken and call for service, sexual or nonsexual, this loss of the slave's right to sleep must be made up for by either allowing him extra sleep in the morning or setting aside a nap time later in the day.

(l) No confining the slave into a space the slave cannot fully lie down in, and no confinement for more than four (4) hours in a week. Also, there is no leaving the slave in such a space that he could not be easily freed from in case of a fire, earthquake, or another emergency. In fact, no such confinement is permissible without a third party present, in case the Master should have a medical emergency.

(m) No full rope bondage, but mummification is acceptable for up to two hours, provided all safety precautions have been made, which includes no mummification without a third party present, in case a second person is needed to release the mummy.[169]

(n) Nothing involving psychological trauma.

(o) No wooden paddles, but leather ones are acceptable.

(p) No cross-dressing by either party.

(q) No single-tailed whips, but floggers are acceptable; and no cats.

(r) No handcuffs behind the slave's back until he is ready for them, but cuffs in front is immediately acceptable.

---

[167] While these may enhance the Master/slave play, asking the emergency room doctor to help with the overenthusiastic results can be embarrassing.

[168] Urophagia: Drinking urine for sexual arousal.

[169] The mummified individual may not be as easily cut out of the mummifying material as may be cutting one free from rope bondage. So, the mummifier must have the necessary tool (surgical scissors, etc.) instantly available.

(s)   No figging[170] or fisting. Finger play is acceptable.

(t)   No prostate milking,[171] but cock milking before some punishment is acceptable.

(u)   No catheterization.[172]

(v)   No toilet paper service without a glove and only for punishment.

(w)   No being humiliated with the name *stupid, idiot, moron,* etc.; every slave should be considered an intelligent person, so any disparaging of that intelligence should be a serious turn-off. Should the Master even accidentally call the slave this, the Master will accept full responsibility and voluntarily wash his own mouth out with soap in the presence of the slave. This will be one of the rare times that the Master takes any punishment for his own deed. Humiliating names such as *bitch-boy, boy-cunt, boot-licker, sub-boy, butt-beaten boy, urine boy, dog, toy,* etc. are acceptable.

(x)   No kind of humiliation from an outside person, unless agreed upon in advance by the Master and slave.

(y)   No making of undue demands on the slave if he is ill.

(z)   Any punishment must always match the offense, and punishments may not be unnecessarily delayed or accumulated. A punishment not given within twenty-four (24) hours of the offense is invalid.

(**VI**) Section six lists the punishments that the slave might be subject to.

(a)   To distinguish genuine punishment from erotic discipline, any punishment by pain or humiliation will be applied when the slave is not likely to be in a sexually aroused state. This usually means that punishment will occur shortly after the slave has been made to ejaculate. While such post-ejaculation punishment might include a spanking, belting, paddling, caning, or flogging, it should only include anal penetration (the Master fucking the slave) without

---

[170] This is inserting a piece of fresh, skinless ginger into the anus or rectum. This creates a strong burning sensation that does not entail permanent damage. It is erotic to some players but can also be used as a punishment.

[171] This is a serious step beyond prostate massage. In this, the simple massage is continued until as much prostate fluid as possible is released. It is an SM technique that some bottoms find pleasurably painful, while others find it just painful.

[172] Urethralism.

the Master offering at least two other reasonable alternatives. Such punishment sex can occur as a result of the slave having no justifiable reason for previously saying no to the Master's sexual advances. None of this will go far enough to break any skin or leave any wound or scar on the slave's body.

(b) For verbal offenses including saying "no" at the wrong time, the slave may receive three (3) safe slaps across both sides of the face; or his mouth washed out with soap, raw lemon juice, or the slave's own urine; or the unaroused slave may be required to piss over the Master's boots and then get down and lick those boots clean; or the slave may have to wear a soft bit, not a gag; or the slave's mouth may be taped over, but a hole must be left for him to drink with a straw; but no such oral punishment for more than two (2) hours; or the slave may be denied a favorite food for as long as the Master sees fit, but never the necessary nutrition to keep the slave healthy.

(c) The slave may be required to eat his meal while standing up or sitting on the floor.

(d) The slave may be subject to a valid criticism in private or in front of another known Master or slave, but not otherwise, as this would amount to ridicule.

(e) Punishment may be administered in front of another Master or slave, but not in front of any other submissive or any vanilla person.

(f) The slave may be required to wear handcuffs and/or ankle restraints for an entire day, but only if the Master is present in the case of an emergency.

(g) The slave may be required to wear a cock cage and stand by as a mere witness as the Master has sex with another submissive, but not more than once in any month.

(h) If the Master believes the slave has been looking at and listening to another Master too attentively, the slave will be required to sleep with his head upon his Master's dry but pee- and cum-stained underwear for a night, to remind the slave on whom his attention should be exclusively focused.

(i) The slave may be required to clean the Master's toilet bowl or bathroom floor.

(j) If the slave knows that he has committed a punishable offense that the Master does not seem to be aware of, although he might be, it is the slave's responsibility to inform the Master of the offense. Not to do so makes for an unworthy slave. Moreover, if the Master should be aware of the offense but has been waiting for the slave to confess and the slave does not do so, the Master has every right to double up on the punishment.

(k) No one of the above punishments may be used more than once in any seven-day period.

(VII) The seventh section deals with finances.

(a) There will be no interference by the Master with regards to the slave's outside employment.

(b) The finances of the Master and slave will in no way be mixed. The Master's savings and debts are his alone, as are those of the slave.[173]

(VIII) The Master will always respect the slave's spiritual practice, which on occasions may take priority over the slave's responsibility to the Master.[174]

(IX) The Master will not bring a second slave or other submissive into this relationship without consulting this slave.[175] The Master may invite a third party, Master or slave, for a night or two of play every few weeks, but no more.

(X) If this slave is to be subject to the authority of another Master, such as a guardian,[176] that Master will be bound by all the items in this contract.

---

[173] See Chapter 38. Finances.

[174] See Chapter 40. Religious or Spiritual Practices.

[175] If a slave is entering a M/s relationship that he expects to be monogamous, then he should change the word "consulting" to "permission."

[176] See Chapter 50. Guardian Master.

(XI) This contract, even after it has been signed by the Master and slave, will not be officially binding until signed by at least two witnesses, at least one chosen by the Master and one chosen by the slave. After such witnessing, any changes in the contract must again be witnessed by no less than two mutually agreed-upon individuals. This will require each witness being given a copy of the signed and witnessed contract.

(XII) This last section covers the conditions under which either the Master or slave can rightly (unilaterally) terminate the contract.

    (a) If either party fails to fulfill all the above sections of this contract, this will result in termination before its due time. However, if such failure can be mutually worked out, then every effort should be made to do so.

    (b) If the Master should ever hit the slave in anger or vice versa, this is an extreme violation and suspends the contract.

    (c) If the slave should lie to the Master and not confess within twenty-four (24) hours, and the Master feels it cannot be dealt with by some appropriate punishment, the contract can be terminated by the Master.

    (d) If the Master lies to the slave and the slave feels it has been serious enough to create a trust issue between him and the Master, the contract can be terminated. However, this should not be done until the Master has been given at least seventy-two (72) hours to prove himself.

    (e) If it can be shown that either party entered into this contract under false pretenses, it can permanently terminate the contract.

Chapter 52

Ending an M/s Relationship

Since both Master and slave are free agents under the law, either can simply tell the other, "I quit." But for those relationships that have gone on for some time, it is rarely that easy. The M/s bond is often so intense that a breakup between the two can be as difficult as that of many heterosexual marriages. For the slave, but sometimes also for the Master, such a breakup can best be described as "abandonment abuse." Naturally, much of this will depend on how much the lives of the Master and slave have been entangled or integrated—emotionally, sexually, financially, etc. It will also depend on whether the slave has retained enough independence to be able to reenter the world without a Master. Finally, much will depend on the reason(s) for the break-up. Did the Master get tired of the relationship? Did the slave? Was it due to Master exhaustion (burnout)? Was it slave exhaustion? Did the Master want to bring another person into the relationship, but the slave did not want this? Did the slave find a more desirable Master? Did the two just outgrow each other? Were there totally outside factors that doomed the relationship?

Short of the relationship ending due to some kind of abuse, it should not be an excuse for bitterness. Like many marriages that end in divorce, M/s breakups can be devastating to one or both parties. Such breakups are too personal and diverse to give much advice about, but two things can help reduce any trauma. First, avoid entering into such a relationship without having learned as much as possible about each other. Too often, what seems to be good sexual compatibility can lead a Master and slave into a premature relationship without either side allowing for time to explore the nonsexual components of that relationship. This will almost guarantee an eventual breakup. Second, make sure that the contract has clearly stated reasons for dissolving the contract. Many M/s couples think that stating such reasons is not being optimistic enough about the future of the relationship and so either do not include such reasons or do so in such vague terms as to allow too much leniency when it comes to a potential breakup. The more precise the reasons given in the contract for dissolution, the better protection there is for the pride of one or both partners.

Chapter 53

First, the Heavy Hand on the Body to Land

It is strongly advised that for any newcomer to the SM Scene, whether a giver (Top/Dom) or taker (bottom/sub), he should avoid any pain-inducing implements and start with nature's very own hand. The reasons for this ought to be fairly obvious.

(1) The open hand (not the fist) rarely does any serious damage to the body it is striking, providing it does not target one of the really sensitive areas like the small of the back, where the kidneys are located. This fact should give both the spanker and the spankee a greater sense of security in the scene.

(2) The very fact that the Top's hand is receiving almost as much impact as the bottom's body puts a natural limit on a spanking scene, since as soon as that hand starts hurting, the bottom gets relief. This is not the case with implements. Spanking also means that the bottom is aware that the Top is literally sharing in some of his pain, and that automatically creates an erotic connection.

(3) Spanking offers direct flesh-to-flesh contact between players that no instrument/toy offers, and this is inherently erotic.

(4) For the Top's hand to touch the bottom's body, he must be closer to the bottom than if the Top was using a belt, cane, paddle, or whip, all of which necessitate a greater distance between the players. Closeness is generally both more assuring and more erotic than is distance, especially to the bottom.

(5) Spanking is such a universal method of erotic discipline and non-erotic discipline (punishment), that most people do not even think of it as SM or anything kinky; therefore, it can be indulged in by many who would not want to be labeled SMers. For adults with children, this can be especially important. The legal system has often taken children away from parents who have been known to be into kinky sex, even though they have kept it secret from their children. But no judge is likely to do that to a mom and dad who are into a private spanking scene with one another. There are simply too many couples who are into this.

(6) It is as cheap as cheap can be. No expensive toys or larger equipment are needed, no dungeon space is called for, just a hand and a butt.[177]

(7) Special care must be taken with the face, however. To simply slap a person in the face can be very problematic. First, the individual may be wearing contact lenses that can be knocked out or dentures that can be damaged or cause damage to the mouth. Second, a hard slap across the face can damage the neck muscles or even the neck vertebrae, so if the right cheek is to be slapped, the slapper should support the left cheek (left side of the jaw) and adjoining neck with his other hand. The reverse would be for a slapping of the left side of the face. Third, slapping someone's face is a much more personal act than slapping a person's butt, and unless a Dom or Master specifically knows that the sub or slave will tolerate this act, the face should be avoided.

---

[177] Thus, no erotic toys for the kids to discover and ask about.

Chapter 54

Floggers and Cats

A flogger is a multi-lash (tailed) whip with flat lashes. A cat (cat-o'-nine-tails) is a multi-lash (tailed) whip with braided lashes that can be flat or round. Floggers can have either narrow or wide lashes. The flogger, with the narrower lashes, gives a relatively superficial stinging sensation, but if used with extreme intensity, it can cut into the skin. Such cuts can easily turn into scars, which only some edge-playing bottoms like to show off.[178] The wider-lash flogger rarely cuts into the skin, but its thudding sensation tends to go deeper into the tissue. Some bottoms like the thudders because such lashes make for an extra mean sound, which adds to their flogging fantasies. But only the shoulders and butt should be so targeted, never the spine or kidney area. Other floggers, especially those with braided (vs. flat) lashes have far more impact on the skin and the muscles below. Caution: I said *muscle below,* not *fat below.* Striking fat can cause a lot more damage than striking muscle.

The other multi-lash toy is the cat-o'-nine-tails. This is a braided instrument that will definitely cut skin more easily than most floggers, unless the flogger being used has a very narrow lash and the Dom is applying it with a heavy hand. Yet once an initial threat from it has been overcome, many masochistic subs and slaves crave it. For a more savage experience, there are floggers or cats that have lashes with small knots on their tips. These guarantee the drawing of blood.

---

[178] See Chapter 33. Going Feral.

Whatever kind of whip is used, both parties should have studied a "no-hitting-zone chart" which, as the name implies, shows where on the back and front of the male and female body no striking instrument, not even the open hand, should target, due to possible orthopedic damage. This will exclude any bony areas of the body (spine, neck, collar bones, head, elbows, kneecaps, shins, and the back of the knees). It should also exclude the area above the kidneys. Basically, this leaves the butt, the thighs, and the upper part of the back on either side of the upper spine. Also, it is always best to flog a person in a standing position, as opposed to the person being flogged while lying down, since the flogger aided by gravity can be far more dangerous.

> Discipline and punishment mean power
> Which can be easily misunderstood.[179]
> Yet, as a part of every life's adventure,
> We can acknowledge it or we cannot.
> Most people will do best to avoid it,
> For what it means they do not have a clue.
> For the slave, they are part of his Master
> And can be a reward that is his due.[180]

---

[179] Remember, discipline means erotic discipline. Punishment means non-erotic discipline.

[180] By the Thrall.

Topics Covered

A

Abandonment of the slave

Abuse of slave or Master

Aftercare

After-rebound syndrome

Age play

Alcohol and drugs

Alpha slave (senior, training)

Altered state of consciousness (ASC)

Asking for the opinion of a slave

Authority element

Authority sex

B

Barebacking

Being in the here and now, the slave

Beta slave

Black leather wings

Blindfolds and hoods

Bondage and other bodily restrictions and safety

BDSM (bondage discipline dominant submissive sadism masochism)

Blood sports

Boy (general)

Boy/boi (of a Daddy)

Boy toy vs. slave

Bottom and bottoming

Bottom disease

Branding

Brat

Burnout, status

Butt or belly slave

C

Canes

Cats (whips)

Child abuse, former

Clothes (Master's/slave's)

Cock and cunt political incorrectness

Collars (slaves').

Contracts

Convenient fiction or noble lie

D

Daddies

layed punishment credit (DPC)

Dependent personality disorder (DPD)

Disabled Master/slave

Discipline (erotic)

Discipline (non-erotic or punishment)

Do-me queen

Dominant (SM and non-SM)

Dominant masochist/submissive sadist

Dominant versus Master

Drugs

E

Edge playing

Electricity

Empowering (erotic) humiliation

Ending an M/s relationship

F

Families, Master/slave
Family situations
Felching
Finances or avoiding financial
    exploitation
Finding a Master, finding a slave
Fire play
Fisting
Floggers and flogging
Force-me queen
Former friends
Full-disclosure contract
Further references

G

Gags
Games Masters play
Games slaves play
Gamma slave
Gloves, wearing
Going feral
Going under
Guardian Master

H

Hair
Hand shaking and other greetings
Harnesses
Humiliation (erotic) vs. ridicule consent

I

Infantilizing

J

Jewelry, Master/slave
Jock straps

K

Kneeling procedures
Kennel (puppy) play

L

Language, empowering vs.
    disempowering
Law, the
Leather
Love and romance

M

Maintaining the M/s relationship
Manipulating the Master
Masochism (slave and non-slave)
Masochist (passive and aggressive)
Master from hell
Mastering from the bottom
Master's name/title, use of
Master/slave trading party
Masters who have Masters and slaves
    who have slaves
Milking the slave
Monogamy (general)
Monogamy, fluid
Mummification
Myth, perfect slave/perfect Master

N

Nudity, slave

O

Obedience
Out-of-body experience
Outside work
Owned/owner

P

Paddles
Pain, erotic
Personal pronouns
Piercings
Pissing ritual ownership
Power exchange
Property of the slave
Property, slave as
Protocol, slave/Master (high,
    medium, low)
Psychotherapy
Punishment (non-erotic discipline),
    painful and non-painful

R

Religious or spiritual practice
Restaurant behavior
Restroom use
Rimming (oral-anal sex)
Risk-aware consensual kink (RACK)

S

Scat (feces)
Sadist (consent/non-consent requiring)
Sadomasochism
Safe, sane, and consensual
Safe sex and body-fluid exchange
Safe word
Self-doubt (Master or slave)
Scene-specific role play
Sensory deprivation
Servant vs. slave
Sex activity, outside
Shaving
Silent alarm partner (SAP)
Slave classification (domestic, natural,
    pet, show, etc.)
Slave-drop
Slave from hell

Slave gaze
Slave identity drift (SID)
Slave legality
Slave pride and Master pride
Slave speech or slave-speak
Sleeping on the floor or in a bed
SM relationship, adversarial
Spanking
Standing, sitting, and walking positions
Status exhaustion of Master or slave
Submissive (SM and non-SM)
Submissive versus slave

T

Tattoos and other bodily modifications
Time out from roles
"To-hell-with-you" fund
Toileting (Daddy-boy).
Top and topping
Top-drop
Top ordering from the bottom
Topping from the bottom
Toys
Transgendered Master/slave
Transvestite Master/slave
Trust
Types of slaves (born, performance, pet,
    sex, working, domestic, show)

U

Undressing and dressing

V

Vanilla sex
Violet wands
V-slave

W

Wannabe slaves
Water sports (urine)
Whips (cats, floggers, etc.)
Why be a slave?

Z

Zen

For Further Reference

Baldwin, Guy. *Ties That Bind* 2nd ed. Los Angeles: Daedalus Publishing Co., 2003.

_____. *SlaveCraft: Roadmaps for Erotic Servitude* 2nd ed. Los Angeles: Daedalus Publishing Co., 2004.

Bannon, Race. *Learning the Ropes: A Basic Guide to Safe and Fun S/M Lovemaking.* San Francisco: Daedalus Publishing Co., 1992.

Bean, Joseph W. *Flogging.* Eugene, OR: Greenery Press, 2000.

_____. *Leathersex: A Guide for the Curious Outsider and the Serious Player* 2nd ed. Los Angeles: Daedalus Publishing, Co., 2003.

Berman, Louis A. *The Puzzle; Exploring the Evolutionary Puzzle of Male Homosexuality.* Wilmette, IL: Godot Press, 2003.

Bond, Jaclyn. *Sexicon: A Sexual Dictionary.* n.p. Nicotext, 2009.

English, David. *The Ritual of Dominance & Submission.* San Bernardino: n.p., 2017.

Goldstein, Robert. *The Wordsworth Dictionary of Sex.* Ware: Wordsworth Editions, Ltd., 1994.

Gordon, David Cole. *Self-Love.* Baltimore: Penguin Books, 1972.

Grateful Slave, A. *SlaveCraft—Roadmaps for Erotic Servitude: Principles, Skills, and Tools* 2nd ed. Los Angeles: Daedalus Publishing Co., 2004.

Jordan, Mark D. *The Invention of Sodomy in Christian Theology*. Chicago: The University of Chicago Press, 1997.

Kinney, Jay. "Pain, Desire, and Transcendence." *Gnosis: A Journal of the Western Inner Tradition*. #43, Spring 1997, 46–53.

Lenius, Steve. *Life, Leather, and the Pursuit of Happiness*. Minneapolis: Nelson Borhek Press, 2010.

Mains, Geoff. *Urban Aboriginals: A Celebration of Leathersexuality* 3rd ed. Los Angeles: Daedalus Publishing Co., 2002.

Ortmann, David M. and Richard A. Sprott. *Sexual Outsiders: Understanding BDSM Sexualities and Communities*. Lanham, 2013.

Reuter, Donald F. *Gay-2-Zee: A Dictionary of Sex, Subtext, and the Sublime*. New York: St. Martin's Griffin, 2006.

Rinella, Jack. *Becoming a Slave: The Theory and Practice of Voluntary Servitude. With Reflections by His Slave Patrick*. Chicago: Rinella Editorial Services, 2005.

_____. *The Complete Slave: Creating and Living an Erotic Dominant/Submissive Lifestyle* 2nd edition. Los Angeles: Daedalus Publishing, 2004.

Rubel, Robert J. *Master/Slave Relations: Handbook of Theory and Practice*. Las Vegas: Nazca Plains Corporation, 2006.

_____. *Protocol Handbook for the Leather Slave: Theory and Practice*. Las Vegas: Nazca Plains Corporation, 2008.

_____ and M. Jen Fairfield. *Master/Slave Mastery—Updated*. Austin: Red 8 Ball Press, 2014.

Schneider, David. *Street Zen: The Life and Work of Issan Dorsey*. Boston: Shambhala, 1993.

SlaveMaster and Slave 7. *Beyond Obedience*. San Bernardino, CA: n.p., 2017.

Slave the Thrall (Norman McClelland). *Tuesday Beyond Lust: A Bizarre Homoerotic Romance*. Bloomington, IN: iUniverse, 2017.

Stein, David with David Schachter. *Ask the Man Who Owns Him: The Real Lives of Gay Masters and Slaves*. New York: Perfectbound Press, 2009.

Thompson, Mark, ed. *Leather Folk: Radical Sex, People, Politics, and Practice*. Los Angeles: Daedalus Publishing Co., 2004.

Vajra Karuna (Norman McClelland). "Zen in Black Leather" in *Queer Dharma: Voices of Gay Buddhists*. San Francisco: Gay Sunshine Press, 1998, 247–252.

Weal, John D. *The Leatherman's Protocol Handbook: A Handbook on "Old Guard" Rituals, Traditions, and Protocols*. Las Vegas: Nazca Plains Corporation, 2010.

Wiseman, Jay. *SM101: A Realistic Introduction*. Eugene, OR: Greenery Press, 1998.

Printed in the United States
By Bookmasters